·BEDSIDE· CRICKET

CHRISTOPHER MARTIN-JENKINS
·BEDSIDE·
CRICKET

HOWZAT?

CORONET BOOKS
Hodder and Stoughton

Copyright © Christopher Martin-Jenkins 1981
First Published in Great Britain 1981
by J. M. Dent & Sons Ltd

Coronet edition 1983
Third impression 1985

British Library C.I.P.

Martin-Jenkins, Christopher
  Bedside cricket
  1. Cricket – Anecdotes, facetiae, satire, etc.
  I. Title
  796.35'8'0207   GV919

  ISBN 0-340-32110-5

Made by Lennard Books,
Mackerye End, Harpenden,
Herts AL 5 5DR

Editor Michael Leitch
Designed by David Pocknell's Company Limited
Production Reynolds Clark Associates Limited

Printed and bound in Great Britain for
Hodder and Stoughton Paperbacks, a
division of Hodder and Stoughton Ltd,
Mill Road, Dunton Green, Sevenoaks,
Kent (Editorial Office: 47 Bedford
Square, London, WC1 3DP) by
Collins, Glasgow

CONTENTS

I know a man who claims to be the only cricketer ever to have scored a hundred before breakfast. He did so in the Sudan where it is rather too hot to play at mid-day!

The same man, Jake Seamer, once played for Somerset at Portsmouth the morning after going to a Commem. Ball at Oxford. His night's sleep did not begin until he reached the dressing-room at Portsmouth at half-past ten. Two and a half hours later he was woken to be told that Somerset were 40 for five and that, although he had been dropped down the order, he must go in next wicket down. He did so and made his way slowly to the wicket, his eyes blinking painfully in the unaccustomed brightness.

Lofty Herman was bowling. Jake, a studious and determined player with spectacles and a prominent nose, pushed forward to the first ball, which he never saw. He somehow got a touch and edged the ball to third man for a single. At the other end he played the same stroke towards a slightly slower red blur, delivered by Alex Kennedy, and he vaguely heard a fizzing through the air before the ball thudded into his pads. Frank Chester turned down the thunderous appeal. The next ball the batsman actually saw, but as he went back his studless boots slipped underneath him and he did a kind of splits. Again ball hit pads; again a loud appeal; this time Chester's finger went up. J.W. Seamer made his way back towards the pavilion, head down, feeling very small and miserable. He gradually became aware that something was making the crowd laugh, but thought nothing of it until he saw the white of the picket fencing before him and looked up to see Herman standing on the square-leg boundary.

'Excuse me, mate', he said, pointing towards cover-point, 'but the pavilion is in *that* direction!'

It is experiences like these, and

characters like Seamer, which have helped to elevate cricket from a thoroughly enjoyable natural recreation into something of a religion for thousands of addicts for whom the game and all that goes with it has a fatal charm. In 1981 I started to do television commentaries on Sundays, having managed in previous years to play the game myself on the majority of Sunday afternoons. When I mentioned to my wife that in future I should have to try to play on Saturdays instead whenever possible she made one of her periodic, but creditably rare, outbursts: 'What about the garden? And the children? And me? And all those games of tennis we were supposed to be having this summer? What about...' She did not go much further. She knows, like a host of other cricketing wives, that she may win some battles but will never win the war! Once hooked on cricket, one is hooked for life. For better, I believe, than for worse.

How do you know if you are addicted? Just before sitting down to write this preface my eye was caught by a headline on the front page of *The Times* containing the word 'Lords'. Not noticing the missing apostrophe, my interest was immediately aroused and I began to read, urgently. I went no further, however, than: 'In the House of Lords yesterday...' This, perhaps, is the test you should apply: you are on the way to being hooked if the word 'Lords', with or without the apostrophe, speaks to you at once of Father Time, the Tavern, the clock-tower, a sloping ground and a tall pavilion of dark-red brick, its floors smelling of polished lino. You are hooked irrevocably if that emotive five-letter word loses its appeal when used in any context other than cricket.

This book is therefore dedicated to all those to whom the word 'Cricket' on the cover stirred more emotions even than the allusion to 'Bed'!

We might as well open from the Nursery End. Whether character is hereditary or environmental is an argument, so far as I know, as yet unresolved.

I'VE GOT A HEADACH TILL FEB (PLEASE DO DISTU

Non-scientists, perhaps, would settle for a bit of both, although there are enough instances in cricket of sons following successful fathers for the hereditary view to be reckoned the safest. In Test cricket alone I believe there are no fewer than twenty-three fathers who played for their country and produced sons who also played the game at the highest level. The cognoscenti might like to try their hand at naming them from memory (they are listed at the end of the chapter).

More remarkable still, two Test-playing fathers each had *two* sons who played Test cricket – Wally Hadlee of New Zealand and Lala Amarnath of India – and several produced sons who played for different countries. Frank Hearne, who played for both England and South Africa

(England first) had a son, George, who played three Tests for South Africa; and the famous Majid Khan, that most gifted member of recent Pakistan sides, is the son of Jehangir Khan of India. Both played for Cambridge, and the father is perhaps best remembered for killing a sparrow with a ball he delivered for Cambridge against M.C.C. at Lord's – T. N. Pearce somehow played the ball while the sparrow dropped dead against the stumps without dislodging the bails. The son is still talked of at Fenner's as being the best University captain of recent times.

It is a sad fact, however, that not all cricketers can play for their country. There are over a quarter of a million active cricketers in Britain each summer, of whom only a tiny proportion have reached Test level or are ever likely to do so. Yet the vast majority once dreamt of wearing a cap with a crown and three lions. The glorious thing is that having failed to fulfil our dreams, there comes to many of us a second chance in life. It happens when she blushes coyly and says: 'Darling, I saw Doctor Davis today…I think there is someone on the way.'

'Darling, that's wonderful news,' you reply. The true test of a cricketer is what you are actually thinking as you say it. Scotsmen may be thinking: *How the hell are we going to afford it?* Philanderers may be thinking: *Where on earth was I six weeks ago – at home or at the Sales Conference in Manchester?* Oklahomans may be thinking: *It'd better look a lot like me.* But a true cricketer will be thinking of bats, balls, stumps, and a seat in the Lord's pavilion as, twenty-five years later, the tiny embryo now nestling cosily within the tummy of his beloved, makes *his* way back to a huge ovation having completed a superlative hundred against Australia.

Actually, the true cricketer will already have begun his dreams a little before this important day in his life has arrived. He will be aware that family planning, like late-cutting or leg-glancing, is a matter of delicate timing. Thus, with a bit of help from Science and The Almighty, he should have been able to ensure that the happy announcement of impending good news will have been máde very early in the cricket season, so that the baby is born a few months before the next season and nothing important is thereby interrupted.

I have to confess personal failure here. Two of our three children arrived in the cricket season. The first, James, at least had been due to come in good time before the First Test at Trent Bridge in 1973. Although the weather was glorious that early June, he evidently preferred the security of the only place he had known and with every day bringing the Test closer, and no sign of him making any move, my dilemma grew greater.

It was, of course, much more worrying for me than for my wife. Very few wives realize what husbands have to go through on these occasions. We heard of a friend who had hastened the arrival of her offspring by going for a vigorous walk around Winkworth Arboretum (in Surrey). So on the Sunday before the Test I hustled her up hill and down dale amongst the splendid trees and gloriously flowering

HANG ON !

rhododendrons and azaleas, oblivious to the disapproving looks of those who thought it cruel to make a pregnant lady walk so fast. It was no good. I had to leave for Trent Bridge on the Wednesday with my promise to be a good modern father – by being present at the birth – under severe trial.

It was a humdinger of a Test match. England made only a modest 250 against good bowling by Bruce Taylor and Dayle, one of Wally Hadlee's two Test-playing sons. (A third son, Barry, played in the Prudential World Cup, but never in a Test, poor chap.) Snow, Arnold and Greig then bowled out New Zealand for only 87. England made 325 in the second innings with centuries by Amiss and Greig before Illingworth declared with eight wickets down, setting New Zealand an apparently impossible 479 to win. I was confident the England bowlers would finish the job quickly and resolve my problem. The New Zealand captain, Bev Congdon, had other ideas, however, making a marvellous 176, and when I was rung up in Nottingham on Monday evening to be told that the baby would no longer wait I was given the decision of missing either a historic Test

HANG ON!

YORKSHIRE

finish or a (personally) historic birth. I was released from my duties, zoomed down the motorway in time to see James delivered by a kindly Irish nun and watched England win by a mere 38 runs next day on television at the nursing-home. Brian Johnston kindly announced the news and a professional astrologer wrote to me (at great length) to predict that James would end up as a...cricket commentator!

Number Two son came two years later in October, prompting the usual remarks from friends about having the opening pair of our cricket eleven, but our daughter was again due perilously close to a Test match, this time the Edgbaston game against India in 1979. Science, however, had advanced, and with the help of some magic tablets to give nature a push, she made it exactly a day before the match began. It was Brian Johnston, again, I think, who announced the news, but curiously enough it was in the same match that Lin Clugston, who makes the announcements at Edgbaston with a greater sense of humour than some, boomed over the public-address system at the end of a tense maiden over: 'Will Mr Arthur Smith of Ashfield Road, Moseley, please return home immediately: his wife has just produced a baby!'

I was reminded of two rather more melancholy announcements made at the seething Bangalore Stadium on M.C.C.'s tour of India in 1976-77. There was a note of extreme urgency in the voice which suddenly barked out, at great volume: 'Will Mr Ranji Patel please return home immediately. His mother is close to expiring.' An hour or so later came a less desperate follow-up. In a pleading voice the Bangalore secretary stated: 'Will Mr Ranji Patel go home now. His mother has expired.' True cricketers will at once recognize the conflict of loyalties: India were close to winning the match at the time. As at life's beginning, so at its end.

Witness, too, the story of the keen batsman in a club match who, seeing a funeral procession passing the ground, held up an arm to delay the bowler and removed his cap until the procession had passed. 'How nice to see some old-fashioned respect for the deceased', remarked the wicket-keeper. 'Well', replied the batsman, 'I suppose it's the least I could do. She *was* my wife.'

As everyone knows, Yorkshire County Cricket Club will only play cricketers born within the county's borders. There are tales of desperate journeys made by expectant mothers to ensure that the birth should happen in the right place. Lord Hawke, captain of the proudest county from 1883-1910 (during which time he led them to eight Championships) and president from 1898-1938, is the most famous exception to the rule. His parents lost the race and he was born in Lincolnshire.

Generally speaking, cricketing fathers who have miscalculated or have failed to plan their family with the detailed care which the best of them apply to building an innings, do not let mid-season arrivals upset their form. I remember a club batsman excelling himself with a brilliant attacking century during the Cranleigh Cricket Week a few years ago. He explained afterwards that his child was expected that afternoon and that all those brilliant strokes had been made in a vain attempt to get himself out!

The immortal 'Silver Billy' Beldam of Hambledon fame had 39 children (28 with his first wife, 11 more with a second partner) but one can be fairly certain that he would have felt that his first duty on those 39 occasions lay on the cricket field. W. G. Grace is equally unlikely to have interrupted an innings to deliver a child: certainly not if there is the remotest truth in the story that on one occasion as he went out to bat he was told to leave immediately to attend a young patient whose temperature was 101 and whose little sister was showing signs of being stricken by the same fever. 'Call on me again,' said W. G. as he adjusted his M.C.C. cap and sallied forth to bat, 'when their temperatures reach 110 for 2.'

FATHER AND SON TEST PLAYERS

Player	No.	Tests Years	Player	No.	Tests Years
L. Amarnath (India)	24	1933–34 to 1952–53	Mansur Ali Khan,		
M. Amarnath (India)	25	1969–70 to 1978	Nawab of Pataudi (India)	46	1961–62 to 1974–75
S. Amarnath (India)	10	1975–76 to 1976–77	(Both captained India)		
W. M. Anderson			M. Jehangir Khan (India)	4	1932 to 1936
(New Zealand)	1	1945–46	Majid Khan (Pakistan)	57	1964 to 1980–81
R. W. Anderson			J. D. Lindsay (South Africa)	3	1947
(New Zealand)	9	1976–77 to 1978	D. T. Lindsay (South Africa)	19	1963–64 to 1969–70
D. K. Gaekwad (India)	11	1952–53 to 1960–61	V. M. H. Mankad (India)	44	1946 to 1958–59
A. D. Gaekwad (India)	6	1974–75 to 1979	A. V. Mankad (India)	22	1969–70 to 1977–78
E. J. Gregory (Australia)	1	1867–77	F. T. Mann (England)	5	1922–23
S. E. Gregory (Australia)	58	1890 to 1912	F. G. Mann (England)	7	1948–49
W. A. Hadlee			(Both captained England)		
(New Zealand)	11	1937 to 1951	Nazar Mohammad (India)	5	1952–53
D. R. Hadlee (New Zealand)	26	1969 to 1977–78	Mudassar Nazar (Pakistan)	19	1978–80
R. J. Hadlee (New Zealand)	35	1973 to 1980–81	A. W. Nourse (South Africa)	45	1902–03 to 1924
J. Hardstaff, Snr (England)	5	1907–08	A. D. Nourse (South Africa)	34	1935 to 1951
J. Hardstaff, Jnr (England)	23	1935 to 1948	J. H. Parks (England)	1	1937
G. A. Headley (West Indies)	22	1929–30 to 1953–54	J. M. Parks (England)	46	1954 to 1968
R. G. A. Headley			O. C. Scott (West Indies)	8	1928 to 1930–31
(West Indies)	?	1973	A. P. H. Scott (West Indies)	1	1952–53
F. Hearne (England)	2	1888–89	F. W. Tate (England)	1	1902
(South Africa)	4	1891–92 to 1895–96	M. W. Tate (England)	39	1924 to 1935
G. A. L. Hearne			C. L. Townsend (England)	2	1899
(South Africa)	3	1922–23 to 1924	D. C. H. Townsend (England)	3	1934 to 1935
L. Hutton (England)	79	1937 to 1955	L. R. Tuckett (South Africa)	1	1913–14
R. A. Hutton (England)	5	1971	L. Tuckett (South Africa)	9	1947 to 1948–49
Iftikhar Ali Khan,			H. G. Vivian (New Zealand)	7	1931 to 1937
Nawab of Pataudi			G. E. Vivian (New Zealand)	5	1965 to 1972
(England)	3	1932–33 to 1934	S. Wazir Ali (India)	7	1932 to 1936
(India)	3	1946	Khalid Wazir (Pakistan)	2	1954

Note: I had completed this chapter shortly before the publication of the 1981 *Wisden* in which Michael Fordham lists not only fathers and sons but also grandparents, great-grandparents and brothers. I bow to Michael's infinite statistical wisdom!

I

f the baby is a boy (it sometimes isn't, and not every girl is destined to be a Molly Hide, a Betty Snowball, an Enid Bakewell or a Rachael Heyhoe-Flint) the keen father carefully studies his infant's eating habits to determine whether he is going to be a right- or left-handed cricketer.

There is a small but definite advantage in becoming a left-hander. Since most players are right-handed, a left-arm bowler operates from an unusual and therefore more awkward angle. Conversely, bowlers used to aiming at right-handed batsmen tend to stray down the leg-side when

SIX AND OUT OF SIGHT
Playing at Guildford, Surrey's captain Errol Holmes once hit a six on to the open top of a double-decker bus. The ball was never seen again.

IT'S ONL
DAD!

bowling against a left-hander. Very occasionally one finds a truly ambidextrous player. Fred Trueman, for example, could throw in almost equally well with his left or his right hand.

Some years ago, there was an outstanding young cricketer in Middlesex club cricket who appeared unexpectedly one season, having recently married and moved south with his firm from the Midlands. Such was his early form that this unknown quantity was soon being picked for the first team in one of the stronger leagues. He scored a brilliant hundred in his first game as a right-handed opener with all the shots, and although for what he called domestic reasons he was available to play only irregularly after that, the committee always selected him when he said he could play. Later in the year his side

FRIENDLY,

had been set a stiff target against the clock and he scored a superb match-winning century batting *left-handed*. When his delighted captain had bought him a beer afterwards he asked him how he decided which way round he was going to bat.

'Oh, it's quite easy,' said our hero, who shall be nameless. 'If I wake up on Saturday morning and my wife is lying on her right side, I bat right-handed. If she is lying on her left side I bat left-handed.'

'What happens if she's lying on her back?' asked the captain.

'Oh, in that case I'm afraid I have to ring you up and say I'm not available.'

This may explain why he never played regular cricket, but by now I am sure he will have produced some budding future players.

From time to time one feels gloomy about the future of the game, yet although County Championship cricket attracts small crowds these days it is always encouraging to see how many schoolboys turn up, at least during the holidays or at weekends. For them the best moments of the day are often the intervals or before and after play when all but the most unenlightened county clubs allow them to play with tennis balls on the beautiful, even outfields of our county grounds. Very often they just play 'catch' or in the absence of a bat a sort of football/cricket with the 'batsman' kicking the ball away on the half-volley. The majority, though, carry their own bats and wield them with some skill and style. The bowlers, like most small boys down the ages, generally run in and hurl the ball down as fast as they can.

Variations of these childhood games are played every summer in gardens, streets and, of course, at the seaside. Go to any British resort and you might imagine that Winston Churchill's wartime exhortation to fight on the beaches referred not to the German enemy but to the Australian one. What joy there is in a game of cricket with a tennis ball – or any hard rubber ball – played on firm sand with any piece of driftwood serving if necessary as the bat or the stumps. The sea usually marks one boundary, and a line level with a fat lady, basking inshore, often provides the other. Frequently a stray dog, or the family's own pet, serves as an extra fielder – shades of the Grace family playing in their orchard in Gloucestershire with one of their dogs, Ponto, acting as a brave and agile close fielder.

Beach cricket ought, indeed, to include the whole family, with mothers and sisters (if less experienced) given more than an equal chance. A generous spirit pervades these games, for there need be none of the disciplines, the firm laws or the harsh penalties for a mistake which can make the real game a stern and nerve-racking business. You are unlucky, for example, to be born into a family which allows anyone to be out first ball. On the other hand, there are rules peculiar to these unofficial games. Few gardens are big enough not to make the 'six and out' rule a necessity. This helps to teach a young cricketer to keep the ball down – but might it also be one small reason for the native caution of so many English players? In the street you may be caught off lamp-posts and in public parks it may be fatal to get a boundary in the rose-bed behind the 'Please Keep Off' sign.

On the beaches you can often be caught out 'one hand, one bounce'. I once saw Ray Illingworth dismissed like that with a dive into the Barbados sand: how it must have hurt his professional dignity! Indeed 'beach cricket' is almost a term of abuse these days amongst professional cricketers who sometimes use the title derisively to describe the tactics necessary for the 40-over John Player League on Sundays. They recognize, at the same time, how many new devotees the Sunday league has attracted, including a huge armchair audience. In any case, it would be surprising if those same professionals had not played beach cricket in their boyhood.

In the West Indies they actually have Beach Cricket leagues with properly organized games played on the very edge of the breaking surf. Here there are no shivers and goosepimples in a bitter wind as there often are on British beaches: just a lovely, tropical warmth. Imagine the glorious freedom of it! Even to a child, all those fierce fast bowlers must seem quite ordinary without a lethal hard leather ball in their hands. This absence of childhood fear is certainly one reason why Caribbean cricketers are so uninhibited. More West Indians than not seem to play the game absolutely naturally, with the basic rules of technique handed down from one generation to another.

Colin Cowdrey, England's most capped player, that gorgeously effortless stroker of a cricket ball, has acknowledged the help so enthusiastically given by the father who had consciously christened his son with the initials M.C.C.

'The most valuable thing he ever did for my cricket was to use his ingenuity in overcoming the natural tendency of infant batsmen to slog every ball on the leg-side. He used to plant me with my back to the side netting of a tennis court and then bowl at me. Sometimes the challenge would be ten-to-win, at others twenty-to-win. But always those runs had to be gathered on the off-side. He never cared how exhaustingly he had to chase about

the court in pursuit of the ball, so long as his four-year-old son was hitting into the covers or past mid-off, or even trying to cut. He also called on the assistance of a little mongrel dog called Patch.'

Many another successful cricketer has told more or less the same story of parental devotion: the difficulty for the father often lies in suffocating his son with too much enthusiasm.

There are also remarkable stories of men who have mastered this complex technical game without any coaching either at home or at school. The peerless Don Bradman – though he was born into a cricket atmosphere and was helped by both his parents (his mother was a left-arm bowler) and his uncles – was nevertheless largely self-taught. He spent hours by himself, totally absorbed, throwing an old golf ball against a wall and striking the rebound with a stump. That lonely practice in the country town of Bowral helped him to capitalize on a natural genius which was further developed by a quite extraordinary discipline, ambition, confidence and sang-froid.

Despite the passion for cricket in India, the top players come almost exclusively from relatively well-to-do families. There have been strenuous efforts, though, in recent years to try to widen the sphere of opportunity. For child cricketers of any nation the first opportunity to play organized cricket comes at school, and here again it is often a matter of luck whether a boy with a feel for the game will get the encouragement he needs. In areas where the roots of the game grow deep the chances are that he will, but there is no guarantee. I know a primary school in Sussex where the headmistress bans cricket bats on the grounds that they are dangerous. At the secondary stage many schools do not have either trained staff or proper equipment and facilities. There ought to be at least two non-turf pitches, one for practice and one for match

play, at every school: they are relatively inexpensive and head teachers should consider them a basic, essential expenditure.

LEFT ELBOW OUT!... ...AND FOLLOW THROUGH!

Good facilities and good teaching are, of course, the main reasons why some British parents still deny themselves many things in order to pay for private education.

Even in the private sector, however, one comes across strange ideas. I know a prep school in the Surrey hills where the school captain was flogged by his headmaster (now deceased) because, having made a duck in a school match, he committed the unpardonable sin of practising his faulty off-drive as he walked back to the pavilion. A former headmaster of Eton, Dr Heath, went further, taking his cane to the entire school eleven when they returned from a defeat by Westminster School.

On the credit side, it was a Clifton schoolboy, A. E. J. Collins, who at the age of 13 in a match played in 1899 between two junior houses, Clarke's and North Town, made the highest-ever cricket score, 628 not out. He made his innings over four afternoons out of a total of 836, the next highest scorer for Clarke's making 42. In the same match he took 11 wickets for 63. He went on to captain Clifton, but from Sandhurst was posted to India, and after scoring 121 and 68 not out for the Old Cliftonians on leave in 1913, probably his last match, he was killed in France in the first year of the war.

The remarkable Collins, immortal through that one innings, must have found the feat impossible to live up to and never at any other time suggested that he was in the class of many other schoolboy players – amongst them J. N. Crawford, Reggie Spooner, A. G. Steel, Bob Barber, Colin Cowdrey and Richard Hutton – who were obviously destined to play Test cricket, so outstanding were they as teenagers. At the age of only eight John Snow, the future Sussex and England fast bowler, went so far as to strike a bet with another future first-class cricketer, Tony Windows, that he would one day play for England. He was always convinced that nothing would stop him doing so. Many of us who fell early under cricket's magical spell had similar hopes, but deep down most of us knew that they were 'such stuff as dreams are made on', now long melted into air.

Club cricket can have its traumas at first for the young cricketer who knows his limitations but loves playing the game.

More often that not it is as difficult for a boy who has recently left school to persuade the adult powers to give him a fair crack of the whip as it is for the aspiring professional at a higher level. Those who have played faithfully for the club over the years may have lost their speed in the field, their fire with the ball or their flair with the bat, but the game means much to them and they have no desire to lose their prime place in the batting order or their expectation of a regular bowl. Often, indeed, the immediate interests of the club are better served by the old-stagers, because it takes time for a young cricketer to adapt to adult cricket.

Everything is very different from the school game. The humour is bawdy. Everyone has his leg pulled. The fast bowlers seem faster – often *are* faster – and are certainly larger and stronger. Pitches are seldom so reliable as a well-tended school pitch. Innocent-looking deliveries bowled by bald-headed men with large paunches turn out to possess hidden devils. Umpires are less predictable. It is not as safe as it looks to take a single to the old boy in the yellowing sweater with a limp:

he turns out to have a throw like a rifle-shot. When an opportunity comes to bowl, the young fast bowler's nasty lifting deliveries are nudged away to the square-leg boundary with the greatest of ease by a batsman who looks as though he's never been taught any technique at all, and the young spinner's subtly flighted off-breaks are driven to all parts by a tall chap in a striped cap who also turns out to be a brilliant hooker and puller whenever the ball is pitched shorter.

It is after the game is finished, however, that the differences are most marked. The school game ends with a rapid change back into uniform and resumption of schoolboy life. But for adults, the day has only just begun when stumps are drawn. From the most bucolic village to the most sophisticated league, the drinks in the bar are what count. There it is that the swanky, loud-mouthed so-and-so of a fast bowler turns out to be a most charming solicitor of high repute, and the self-effacing batsman who never said a word when he was given out caught behind off the buckle of his pad emerges as a brilliant raconteur of blue stories. There it is that players who have not had much luck slowly drown the pain of failure, while those who have done well in the match discuss over and over again the three cover-driven fours in one over which turned the game – 'You can bat in your sleep on this pitch' – or the brilliant catch which was 'just one of those ones which stuck'. A marvellous cameraderie spreads around friend and foe.

Two decades ago the cheerful swapping of stories, post-mortems on the game, discussions on why England's Test team was such a dead loss and sundry other meanderings round a cricket theme used invariably to take place in the pub. Nowadays even small village clubs raise money by fetes, whist-drives, raffles, donkey-derbies and celebrity matches, and perhaps a loan from the National Playing Fields Association in order to build

themselves a bar. It isn't really quite the same, but the takings at the bar help to keep down match-fees to a feasible level. There are more women to be seen drinking with the cricketers these days, too, although they tend to be either starry-eyed fiancées who have not yet learned to be bitter about how much cricket their beloved plays, or more elderly wives whose children have left the nest and who long ago gave up trying to persuade the old man that there are other ways to spend a warm Saturday evening in summer than sinking pint after pint of bitter from the 'jug'.

The jug, filled up first by the home skipper, then by the opposing captain, circulates briskly. Traditionally, anyone who has got five wickets or fifty runs also pays for a jug, so it is a bad evening, or rather a bad match, if it doesn't get filled up at least six times.

To a temperate youth all this takes some getting used to, but playing club cricket at any level means accepting that it is a man's world. It is not – or not usually – a case of a cricket match being an excuse for lingering on after the match to talk about cricket. Perhaps there are indeed better things to do on summer evenings but there are worse things too, as any policeman will tell you, and drinks with the opposition after the game are a part of the ritual. They help to give cricket its unique character and friendliness. The tradition goes back to the earliest days: any student of Hambledon will know how important was the Bat and Ball Inn besides Broadhalfpenny Down to those larger-than-life characters who played in the club's great days of the 1770s and 1780s. Indeed the club's 'head and right arm', Richard Nyren, was the innkeeper and the inn, in effect, was the clubhouse:
'Then fill up your glass, he's the best that drinks most.
Here's the Hambledon Club! – who refuses the toast?'
In more recent times fear of the

breathalyzer has happily prevented many excesses, and the lure of television along with the emancipation of women, and in many cases the pressures of work, have cut down the time spent at the club bar. But cricket maintains its genuine social role: in James Pycroft's Victorian novel *Elkerton Rectory,* the Reverend Henry Austin records:

'My cricket club was designed to encourage sympathy between man and man, however wide their ranks might be asunder, and most admirably did it conduce towards this end.'

It still does, although village cricket these days embraces a wider range of professions than it used to. It is many years now since a batsman walked out in a village match in Somerset with the club's only pad strapped to his right leg instead of his left. 'Bert', said the opposing village's fast bowler when he saw one of his old adversaries thus clad, 'you've got your pad on the wrong leg.'

'Ah', said Bert, in all seriousness. 'So I 'ave. But t'will be on the right one when I get up t'other end.'

ENTER THE LEAGUES

League cricket used to be the prerogative of the Midlands and North of England. Through the determination of the former England batsman Raman Subba Row and others, the majority of clubs in the South also joined or formed leagues during the 1970s.

In Scotland, Ireland and Wales too the main clubs are engaged in league cricket on most Saturdays of the season. It is only recently that the public in England have been made aware how seriously the game is taken in certain pockets of the Celtic lands, because of the participation of Scotland and Ireland in the Benson and Hedges Cup and the National Westminster Bank Trophy (not to mention Wales in the Prudential World Cup). But Scottish cricketers have long been proud of producing England Test players of the class of Douglas Jardine, Ian Peebles and Mike

Denness, and Ireland rightly look back with pride at bowling out the 1969 West Indies touring team for 25 at Londonderry (Goodwin 5 for 6, O'Riordon 4 for 18).

The image of league cricket in the North is of a grim, tough contest. The first adjective sometimes applies perhaps, the second almost always – especially in those leagues where professional cricketers are employed each season to supplement the local amateur talent. Most of the great West Indian fast bowlers have terrorized opposing batsmen in Northern England in their time, notably in the Lancashire and Central Lancashire Leagues where overseas stars can often make as much money for less work than in county cricket.

Of the many West Indians who have graced the Northern leagues over the years the most famous association was that between Learie Constantine and Nelson, whose public flocked each weekend in large numbers to see their glittering acquisition from faraway Trinidad justifying not only his large salary but also, as often as not, the traditional collection round the ground which acknowledges to this day a fifty, a hundred or a good piece of bowling.

If a local cricketer does well in this sort of company it is not long before the committees of Lancashire, Yorkshire, Derbyshire, Staffordshire or the other traditional heartlands of league cricket are making inquiries. Now that strong leagues are established in the Southern counties as well, there is less chance of outstanding ability wasting its sweetness on the desert air. Since most of the matches are played under limited-over rules, however, league cricket has become more predictable and the trends – as with the counties – are towards much improved fielding, defensive tactics and bowling designed to save runs rather than take wickets.

THE VILLAGE GREEN

Even village clubs have been drawn into leagues in recent years, but the essential character of village cricket has not, happily, been lost. After all, village cricket, though it may have been laughed at from outside,

has always been a very serious business for those taking part.

A few seasons ago a City investment analyst named Tim Lowdon was walking his dog round the village green at Whitchurch in Hampshire one Sunday morning. He was hailed by the village captain who, knowing him to be a keen cricketer, asked him to make up the numbers that afternoon as they were one short. Tim came in to bat at number eleven later in the day with Whitchurch in a spot of trouble at nought for nine! With great aplomb he scored a single off the first ball he received to get the scoreboard, if a trifle belatedly, moving. Unfortunately his partner was less fortunate and the home team were dismissed for one. The glorious uncertainty of cricket is never so uncertain or so glorious as it is on the village green where the game first came to be played in an organized form around the 17th century in the Weald of Southern England.

Much of the comedy of village cricket lies in its very seriousness. For every husky, untutored blacksmith breasting the brow of the hill, or paunchy publican labouring after the ball in the outfield with more concern for his lumbago than for saving the four, there are two at least in the side who see in every village game a Test match. Their dress and equipment are correct, and unlike the others they do not rely on the soiled and inadequate collection of old bats, non-matching pads and gloves and festering boxes which litter one corner of the dressing-room. In the field they rub their hands before every ball, get down low in the slips or move in briskly from the covers as each ball is bowled. At the crease, regardless of ability, they chew gum assiduously to aid their concentration, prod the pitch and touch the peak of their cap after each ball, look amazed if they are beaten, even more so if they are bowled and quite outraged if they are given out l.b.w.

One such character was given out l.b.w. one day when the ball struck him on the chest. Striding furiously past the umpire he muttered that it could not possibly have been out. 'You look in the local paper on Friday and see if it was out or not', said the umpire. 'No, *you* look', was the biting riposte, 'I'm the editor.'

Some of the more unexpected and amusing incidents occur when village teams meet grander and more pretentious ones. On a recent tour of the West Country a wandering team lost their first wicket early against a rustic Somerset side but were unworried because they had an outstanding batsman who had scored a good many runs for Oxford against strong county attacks earlier in the summer. He walked out slowly, twirling a top-quality bat and adjusting the peak of his Oxford cap. The first ball was outside the off-stump and popped a bit and our hero elegantly shouldered arms, then strolled down the pitch to flick away a sod of earth near where the ball had pitched. At once the wicket-keeper threw down the stumps, appealed and the square-leg umpire raised his finger with alacrity and a smile which seemed to say: 'That'll teach the swanky bastard'.

The funniest end to any match I have played in occurred when a village team, again with some help from the umpire, had hurtled through a London school Old Boys side full of talented players. There was nothing for it but to play for a draw. The opposing captain, a Cambridge Blue this time, played three successive maiden overs against the village club's off-spinner and duly pushed safely forward to the first five balls of the final over. The last ball was tossed right up and the batsman pushed even more carefully forward, his bat angled correctly over the ball. Yet somehow it spun very slowly back under the bat, trickled towards the wicket and gently removed one bail!

The professions of village cricketers these days are much more varied than they were in the days before trains and motor cars when the landlord, the parson and the squire, supplemented perhaps in larger communities by a solicitor or a doctor, were surrounded mainly by those who worked on the land or with animals. A village I know well in West Surrey has a useful spin bowler who unfortunately has to miss a season every now and then because he is continually being caught climbing up ladders against the walls of country houses at night. He has recently turned over a new leaf and has had two successful seasons, although he did show special pleasure last summer when told that the opposing batsman he had just had stumped was a policeman!

Humiliating experiences such as that suffered by Whitchurch are common enough in minor cricket. Well in excess of a hundred instances of sides being bowled out for nought have been recorded, the most recent possibly being the game between Red Triangle Second XI and Tarleton Second XI in the Fourth Division of the Southport and District League in 1980. Having been bowled out for nought Red Triangle lost the match to a leg-bye scored from the seventh ball of the Tarleton innings; their captain, Tony Quinn, immediately resigned. In the following game, however, against the Y.M.C.A. Second XI, Red Triangle scored 183 then bowled their opponents out for 19, one 'Taffy' Clegg taking seven for 16.

A similar experience had been suffered by Bexley in Kent in 1884. They were bowled out for seven by Orleans Club, for whom one F. R. Spofforth – the demon himself – took seven for two in 27 balls, but a few games later they scored 402 for no wicket, John Shuter making 304 not out, against Emeriti C.C.

There are, incidentally, at least seven authenticated instances of bowlers taking all ten wickets for no runs. They were listed by E.K. Gross in Volume Three of the *Journal* of the Cricket Society,

starting with A. Dartnell, a draper by trade and Methodist by religion, who took all ten for none for Broad Green against Thornton Heath at Croydon in Surrey in 1867.

The term 'village', in the sense of a small rural community, sadly applies strictly now to only a very few of the thousands of cricket clubs of Britain; but more than seven hundred, defined as rural communities of not more than 2,500 inhabitants, contest each year the Whitbread Village Championship organized by *The Cricketer.*

The essence of village and league cricket lies not in statistics but in people. Most clubs are based round a few dedicated characters like the former club captain who tends the pitch through the week, rolls it until it is dark on Friday night, marks out the creases on Saturday morning and watches philosophically through the smoke from his pipe as the rain begins to fall at a quarter to two. He is complemented by the younger man who starts phoning round the members on Monday night, finds eleven fit and willing men by Thursday, replaces two of them because they have dropped out on Friday, captains the side on Saturday and Sunday, as often as not making most of the runs or taking a good many of the wickets, serves behind the bar after the match, cleans up when most of his mates have gone and reminds his wife when he gets back home that an extra tea will be needed for the Colts match on Wednesday. The sleepy, eternally loyal, reply comes back: 'Ah, and don't *you* forget the Committee meeting on Tuesday to discuss the President's match. And the Donkey Derby to raise the money for that new sightscreen . . . and for that new fridge in the kitchen.'

Even as late as 1947 there were gentlemen who could spend most of their summers playing cricket.

One such was 'Bushy' O'Callaghan, who played for many clubs, including the Cryptics, a wandering club most of whose members are schoolmasters. Despite playing almost every day from April to October in the hot summer of 1947, he just failed to emulate Denis Compton and Bill Edrich, who that year each scored 3,000 runs. He therefore organized a special match on New Year's Eve and duly reached the magic figure.

There are wandering clubs and wandering clubs but generally speaking they cater for the more exclusive sort of club cricketer. I should be more explicit: generally they make no apology for the fact that the majority of their members are cricketing sons of the public schools and jealously maintain their right to be exclusive. They seldom turn out a bad side; their colours are almost always a combination of gaudy stripes; they are usually full of gifted and expansive stroke-players but a bit short of quick bowling. They believe that a proper game of cricket on a single day has a declaration by the first side at anything over 200 no later than halfway through the match with the second side getting the runs in the last over or losing their last wicket instead in a gallant but vain attempt.

This may be considered a somewhat old-fashioned approach in the days of Saturday league cricket. However, because of this generous attitude to the game, a throwback almost to the Golden

Age and certainly to the now almost vanished era of country-house cricket, one seldom plays in a bad game when two wandering clubs are involved.

They may be school Old Boys sides such as those who contest *The Cricketer* Cup each year; university offshoots like the Quidnuncs or the Harlequins; service sides like the Green Jackets; county-based clubs like the Band of Brothers, Yorkshire Gentlemen, Sussex Martlets, Hampshire Hogs, Devon Dumplings, Gloucestershire Gypsies, etc; or long-standing privately formed clubs like I Zingari, Free Foresters, Incogniti, Arabs, Buccaneers, Stoics, Cryptics, Romany, Yellowhammers and many others. Indeed one seldom plays in a bad game when only *one* side is one of these famous wanderers because their approach always seems to bring out the best in opposing clubs, most of whom are now bound by the 'play for points' mentality of Saturday league cricket. They often discover on Sunday that a pitch upon which 150 runs seemed a desperate struggle to get on Saturday has suddenly become a 'belter.'

WHO WAS WISDEN?

The founder of the revered *Cricketer's Almanack*, John Wisden (1826–84) has another if lesser-known claim to fame as the smallest fast bowler ever. He was 5ft 4in tall and weighed only 7 stone. A Sussex regular, Wisden's greatest achievement on the field happened in 1850 when he took all 10 wickets for South v. North.

These clubs of proud traditions, full as they are of university Blues, Etonians, military officers and double-barrelled names, may be exclusive by nature, but the majority of their members are at ease in any sort of cricket below first-class level and many of the active younger members would not be satisfied if they did not mix their wandering cricket with some club or village games in which the competitive spirit is that much tougher and meaner. This is not to say that wandering cricket is not keenly contested. The standard is invariably very high, apart from some languid fielding on occasion and a paucity of good fast bowlers. Moreover one seldom comes across a cricketer in these games who is not knowledgeable about the game and almost never one who is not gifted in at least one department of it. For me wandering cricket means good company, good wickets, players out to enjoy the game and the near-certainty that everyone will have a sense of the game's ethical traditions, a knowledge of the basic technical rules, and a certain cricket know-how that prevents them, for example, from standing in no man's land in the outfield of a small ground, too deep to save the one and too close to catch the skier or cut off the four.

This was not always so. Alec Waugh once recalled the captain of the now-defunct Chiltern Ramblers, who had flourished in the 1920s when club cricket was more leisurely and more varied in standard than it is now. The Chiltern Ramblers could call upon players of the calibre of R.H. Bettington of Oxford, Middlesex and New South Wales, for first-class cricketers played a good deal of club cricket then but now seldom have the chance or the inclination. However, they were captained by a barrister named E.E. Carus-Wilson. Waugh wrote of him:

'He was tall, elegant, sandy-haired. He looked a cricketer. He would walk to the wicket with a firm, confident stride. He would take guard, look round, settle his stance. Then as the bowler's arm went over, he would lift his bat; his left leg would go down the wicket; his left elbow would face the bowler; his bat would follow his leg: a copybook forward stroke. But the ball would miss the bat. I never saw him make a run . . . He would field at mid-on. I do not remember seeing him hold a catch?

The ladies, and ladies is the word, have more of a part to play in wandering cricket than they do in other forms of the club game. It is not that they do the teas or anything like that: but they are a part of the elegant scene, their dresses and hats, pretty faces and lissom figures drawing the eye from the striped blazers, and their good breeding and intelligence helping to divert conversation away from strictly cricketing matters onto broader plains.

Sometimes etiquette can be taken to excess. At a match in Kent between two wandering clubs a few seasons ago, a batsman was badly hurt early in the game when he tried to hook a ball and 'top-edged' it into his face. Seeing him prostrate on the ground, bleeding profusely, the president of the fielding side, who was playing in the game, hastily summoned his wife from their Jaguar on the boundary's edge. 'Bring the first aid kit, dear, quickly,' he called.

The president's wife, smartly dressed, hurried out to the middle carrying a tin of plasters, ointments and bandages. Gratefully the stricken batsman half-raised his wounded head from the ground. 'Oh, I'm sorry,' said the president quickly. 'I don't think you've met my wife. Diana, this is Nigel Tapscott-Jones . . .'

Since there is little point in joining a club unless you play for it, you have to be careful as a keen young cricketer not to be tempted too often by the prestige of a famous tie. Yet it is difficult to resist the honour of joining I Zingari (founded in July 1845 by J.L. Baldwin, R.P. Long, Sir Ponsonby Fane and the Hon. Frederick Ponsonby, later Lord Bessborough) especially when the letter informing you of your election is conveyed by a knight on behalf of a peer of the realm who was once prime minister!

Another of the pleasures of wandering cricket is that the clubs have a knack of searching out not only good batting wickets but also some of the most beautiful grounds. The best of them all, without doubt, is Arundel, in the lee of the castle with its majestic arboreal variety and its long views across the South Downs. Within the space of a few months I was fortunate enough to play one match for the Foresters against the Australian IZ at their New South Wales ground at Camden Park, seat of the Macarthur-Onslows; and another at Arundel for the Arabs against Lavinia, Duchess of Norfolk's Eleven. The first match, in February, was played in a temperature of 110°F. For the second, in May, the thermometer struggled to reach 50. Both were well-fought cricket matches played in an atmosphere of civilized enjoyment.

If anyone is surprised to read that country-house cricket exists in Australia, he or she may also be interested to know that it once flourished in Hollywood in the days when the former England cricketer C.A. Smith was playing his permanent role as the archetypal English gentleman. As he grew older, however, Sir Aubrey's eyesight began to fail and to his embarrassment he dropped a simple slip catch one day during one of the games over which he would preside with much majesty. Instantly he stopped the game and called for his butler, who walked slowly onto the ground and bowed low.

'Bring me my glasses', commanded Sir Aubrey.

With due ceremony the butler left the field and returned a few moments later with a pair of spectacles on a silver salver. Sir Aubrey put them on and signalled to the umpires that they might resume play. The bowler tore in again, refreshed by the break. The batsman pushed timorously forward, edged the ball and watched as Sir Aubrey juggled vainly with the catch and dropped it. Picking up the ball in fury he yelled across to the watching butler:

'Hetherington you idiot, you brought my *reading* glasses!'

There is another 'cricketing butler' story concerning the Duke of Norfolk who, shortly before a match between his side and the Sussex Martlets at Arundel, discovered that there was only one umpire. He asked his butler, Summers, to do the vacant job. Unfortunately, when the Duke was batting his partner called him for a short single and the great man slipped in the middle of the pitch. In the heat of battle his identity was forgotten and the Duke was easily beaten by the return to the wicket-keeper. There was a loud instinctive appeal of 'How's that?' from the fielding side. Acute embarrassment for Summers: would he give his Master out? After a long pause he was asked by the nearest fielder: 'Well, is he in or out?

Summers replied with impressive dignity: 'His Grace is not in.'

The Duke was the keenest of cricketers. Apart from his presidency of Sussex, the Duke was manager of the 1962–63 M.C.C. tour of Australia, with Alec Bedser as his assistant. The Duke's grasp of mundane financial matters was found to be somewhat limited when he took the side to Kalgoorlie for a country fixture whilst Bedser stayed in Perth for net practice with some of the other players. Bedser had given the Duke the tour cheque book with the request that he should pay the hotel bill and record the full details. When the Duke returned he handed back the cheque book, saying that he had thrown away the bill but the details were all recorded on the counterfoil. Bedser looked inside and saw on the counterfoil the single word: 'Kalgoorlie.'

In all other respects his Grace was a very successful manager, and there is another charming story told of that tour. The Duke and Duchess were visiting another country match and a local schoolgirl was given the honour of presenting a posy of flowers to the Duchess. Just before she did so her headmistress reminded her: 'Don't forget to say "Your Grace".' The little girl went shyly up to the Duchess, curtsied and said: 'For what we are about to receive, may the Lord make us truly thankful.'

The most famous example of the humour of cricket crowds was the admonition by one Aussie barracker to the unpopular England captain Douglas Jardine on the 'bodyline tour' of 1932-33.

It was a hot day and the flies were constantly buzzing around the captain's immortal Harlequin cap. As he swatted energetically at one particularly persistent gnat a voice, which had been administering advice to the players all day, rose again above the hubbub: 'And keep yer bloody hands off our flies, Jardine.'

Amateur cricket is for players first, spectators second, but there is a good case for that order of precedence to be reversed if the game is to continue as a professional sport. All too often players (and umpires) who ultimately rely upon spectators to pay their wages break faith with them by looking too concerned about getting back to the dressing-room in uninviting weather conditions. Sometimes, of course, it is an illusion: playing conditions may be genuinely impossible when the sun has come out after rain – even though there is no reason apparent to inadequately informed spectators why cricket is not taking place. Bad public relations and a failure by players and umpires to be seen to be doing their best to get the game going are often to blame for the crowd fury which leads to riots amongst volatile onlookers like those in the Caribbean and to the kind of fracas which demeaned the Saturday of the Centenary Test at Lord's in 1980.

It is usually the occasional cricket watchers, not the regulars, who make most noise. At such disappointing moments the hardened spectators, at least in England, tend to react with a philosophical smile. The real devotees – those faithful zealots who spend much of their summer watching county cricket and many of their winter evenings talking about the game as members of their local cricket society – are well prepared for rain. An umbrella goes up, a plastic macintosh is unrolled and put on, a cheese roll comes out of the basket and a book on cricket is read or the crossword patiently attended to until the fatal announcement that there will be no further play today.

Spectators reflect the region or country they come from more clearly than players. One Southern enthusiast up to watch a Test in Leeds was unwise enough to go off to get a sandwich and a beer at lunchtime, leaving his hat on his seat to show that it was taken. When he got back a thick-set miner was firmly established and no other space was visible. The hat was on the ground near the miner's large black boots. 'Excuse me', said the Southerner politely, 'but I think you are sitting in my seat by mistake. That's my hat.' The miner fixed him with an icy stare and replied: 'Up 'ere lad, it's bums what bags seats, not 'ats.'

The cricket supporters of Yorkshire are second to none in their enthusiasm for and knowledge of the game. They can take a bit of time to get to know you, though. I have kindly been asked to make several visits to address the famous Wombwell Cricket Lovers Society, which is run from Barnsley with breathless energy by their secretary Jack Sokell. On my first visit I was presented with a handsome glass mug on which a local artist had cleverly engraved a very good likeness of my face. Attempting to break the ice, I began my talk by saying: 'First I must thank you all for presenting me with this ugly mug.' I meant, of course, my own, but as I looked along the serried ranks of sturdy miners, not a flicker of amusement showed on any face.

Nothing so inhibits a speaker as one of his jokes going down like a lead balloon, but the first impression was wrong. I soon found out that the men (and a few women) of the Wombwell society are warm people with a lively sense of humour. So too are the members of the Northern Cricket Society, the Sheffield Cricket Lovers, the Lancashire, the Stourbridge, the Hampshire, the Essex . . . The movement has grown rapidly in recent years, all over Britain and in one or two other countries too. The Cricket Society itself, father of them all, now has some 2,200 members. Their members are the

faithful souls who would rather go without bread than give up membership of their county club and who make sure, when England are touring Australia, that the alarm is set to go off five minutes before the early morning broadcast begins. No doubt that same philosophical smile greets every England collapse.

Some of the more wealthy or adventurous of this ilk have in recent years taken to spending their holidays watching M.C.C. – or England, as they now are – battling it out overseas. The players do not wholly approve. Whereas their leisure activities off the field used to be watched in the old days by a few journalists, they are now also under scrutiny from critical holiday-makers, some of whom think it wrong if the players are not in the nets all day and living quiet, abstemious lives by

night. Even journalists sometimes feel that their private reserve has been intruded upon. These people should be back at home reading and listening, not coming out to see for themselves! This may sound a mean and illogical feeling, but I can only say that I have shared it, in a way it is because a cosy party has been invaded, and also because people joining a tour for only a fortnight or so tend to make instant judgments about what is going on without knowing the whole picture.

In the 1981 Barbardos Test a whole stand at the Kensington Oval was filled with British supporters and it was said that half the rest of the crowd were relatives of Roland Butcher! It was different when only a few could afford to follow the tour. The 1970–71 series in Australia was watched from first match to last by two well-to-do

English gentlemen, John Gardiner and Geoffrey Saulez. The former became the driving force behind the 'I.C.C. Trophy' which brought the little cricket nations of the world to England to play in the World Cup, and the latter has since become England's regular scorer on overseas tours, paying most of his own expenses. So fanatical is Geoffrey Saulez that he scores for Pakistan or the West Indies or any country that will have him when his own is inactive.

He is a large, intelligent man with a nose like that of Mr Punch and he sometimes terrorizes fellow-scorers during matches overseas if they do not come up to his high standards. He also reads every hotel bill with the same fastidiousness and usually finds an error! He is probably the

ultimate cricket spectator because I believe he must see more cricket matches each year than any living man.

Australian spectators have a reputation for the quick-witted piece of barracking which happily the mindless yelling of thousands of okkers in recent seasons has not altogether snuffed out. The first time Derek Randall batted in Australia after this triumph in the Centenary Test in Melbourne was in a country match early in the 1978–79 tour. He studiously played a maiden over, whereupon a bearded man near to where I was walking round the boundary put down his can of beer, cupped his hands and shouted: 'Aw, come on, Randall, you couldn't get a kick out of an electric chair!'

It was on the previous tour that Colin Cowdrey had come bravely out to face the fury of Lillee and Thomson exactly twenty years after taking on Lindwall and Miller on his first tour. As the first of many bouncers whistled past Cowdrey's left shoulder an encouraging voice said: 'That's the spirit, Thommo, rattle out a tune on his false teeth!'

All Pommy players are fair game. Trevor Bailey, who used to win grudging admiration from Australian crowds for his bloody-minded batting, had a habit of bowling one imaginary ball when he came on to bowl in order to get his run-up correct. He did this when England took the new ball ten minutes from the end of the day at Brisbane in 1954, Australia having lost only two wickets in humid heat. As he completed his practice run a man shouted: 'And that's the best bloody ball you've bowled all day, Boiley.'

Freddie Brown got the treatment on the previous tour. He had been front-page news one morning after hitting a lamp standard in a car the previous night. When a wild swipe at a Lindwall outswinger failed to make contact by some distance the reaction was swift, if predictable: 'Pity you didn't miss the lamp too, Brownie.'

Another England captain, J.W.H.T. Douglas, whose initials the Melbourne crowd believed stood for 'Johnny Won't Hit Today,' drew the agonized plea during a long, defensive innings: 'Fetch a cop someone and pinch that bugger for loitering.' And Trevor Bailey, batting at Sydney, was once asked two pertinent questions: 'Why don't you drop dead Boiley? Or are you?' When it comes to slow play, in fact, Australians themselves do not escape. 'Slasher' Mackay, Queensland's stubborn left-hander, was told by a bored spectator: 'Blimey Mackay, you'll never die of a stroke,' and Jimmy Burke was informed during a patient rearguard action: 'Burke, you're like a bloody statue. I wish I was a pigeon.'

'Yabba,' the humourist of the Sydney Hill before World War II, used to be an entertainment in himself. He it was, I believe, who first suggested to a bowler who was continually beating the bat: 'Send 'im down a grand piano, mate, and see if he can play that!' To less successful bowlers he would yell: 'Yer length is lousy but yer *width*'s pretty good.' When Charles Kelleway took a long time to get off the mark and finally did so with a quick single he shouted: 'Whoa there, he's bolted.' And when Maurice Tate, always having trouble with his boots, bent once again to do up his laces, Yabba called: 'Thank goodness he's not a flaming centipede.'

But the last word shall be with an English spectator. In the Lord's Pavilion they tend to be either very knowledgeable or very ignorant about the game. The Lord's Taverners once had a match at headquarters during which Norman Wisdom got himself into a succession of hilarious running tangles in partnership with Roy Castle. An elderly gentleman with a moustache and panama hat, obviously not quite sure what match he was watching, turned to his neighbour with a half-smile and said: 'That chap ought to be a comedian, y'know.'

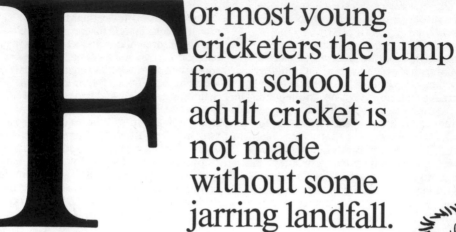

For most young cricketers the jump from school to adult cricket is not made without some jarring landfall.

For 16- and 17-years-olds the shock of playing competitively with adults can be quite severe, both physically and psychologically, not least for the promising youngster who aspires to county cricket. Nowadays it may be less daunting for some than it used to be partly because the young are no longer brought up to believe that all elders are betters. Moreover, most counties now have teams at various age-levels so that an improving player can move by logical stages up the pyramid. This has been the case in Australia, where the grade system toughens the competitive instincts by giving each player one higher step to aim for all the way from country team to the Test eleven.

Even after the abolition of distinctions between amateur and professional cricketers in England after 1962, it took some time for the system to change at junior level. What still tended to happen was that good young school cricketers were seen either as potential members of the county staff, or as 'Young Amateurs', probably bound for university. Young amateur cricket was fun, although there was always the apprehension, not present in schools games, of having to play with team-mates one had only just met.

Arthur McIntyre, coach at The Oval for many years, used to take a keen interest in Y.A. games, although he was sparing with his praise and sometimes caustic in his criticism in the old professional tradition that nothing should be easily gained. When it came to playing Club-and-Ground cricket – matches played by representative county elevens against the best clubs – and occasional Second XI matches, the young amateur with little chance of ever making the county team tended to find himself going in at number seven with little hope, on good wickets, of getting a proper bat, and the all-rounder usually got a bowl only when the regulars

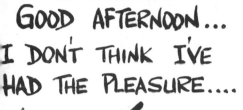

GOOD AFTERNOON...
I DON'T THINK I'VE
HAD THE PLEASURE....

were tired or a long stand was in progress. I once dismissed Alvin Kallicharran for 94 with a long hop at The Oval in just such circumstances. Rightly, no doubt, I was immediately taken off on the grounds that lightning never strikes twice in the same place!

THE CATCH THAT NEVER WAS

So convinced was J. Southerton (Surrey) that a skier he struck against M.C.C. Club and Ground in 1870 would be caught, he set off for the pavilion without waiting to see whether the fielder would safely take it. In fact he dropped it, and the scorebook records the innings as:

'J. Southerton – retired, thinking he was caught – 0.'

To become a professional cricketer requires dedication. Those Young Amateurs of the '60s who were unable to go to university when the academic demands became greater, often found that it was easier to mix with other members of the county staff if they cast off any evidence of their privileged public-school education. But whatever their background those who aspire to play cricket for a living have always had to go through a tough apprenticeship. Old pros will tell you how easy it is nowadays compared with former times when a good deal more time was spent in the nets, tirelessly working on techniques of batting and bowling, and when rewards were smaller and less easily gained. This is undoubtedly so, but the modern county cricketer has to cope with a variety of different cricket tempos – from the three-day fox-trot through the 60-over quick-step to the 40-over Charleston. The experienced South African giant Vintcent Van der Bijl, who had such a successful season for Middlesex in 1980, thought it a daunting task for the young player to 'adapt like a seasoned professional to the many types of wickets and conditions against not only players of England but international players from overseas'.

All but the occasional prodigy, like a David Gower or an Ian Botham (and even they have had lean times at county level) must be very patient and long-suffering. The path to glory, and affluence through a tax-free benefit, is often made with bare feet through nettles. It is much more than simply a question of the nervous feeling in the pit of the stomach when the young cricketer goes to a major county ground to share a dressing-room with players he may have adulated only a year or two before. It is a lad of strange confidence who at first does not feel out of place and out of his depth. These feelings soon pass and most people relax, encouraged by the feeling that they have grown up, cheered also by the banter

SORRY MR McINTYRE!

which goes on in any dressing-room. The real test of character comes when keen and gifted young players, anxious to get to the top, quickly find themselves spending season after season as Second XI cricketers. Rivalry for the rare chances to play a game or two in the First XI – even if it is only in a limited-over game – can become bitter as the season wears on and the fateful day draws near, towards the end of August, when the county's committee make their decision about who will and who will not be retained on the staff. Often it is a hit and miss business and only the genius is certain of a quick rise to the top.

I remember Geoff Howarth, for example, now a highly successful Test batsman and captain, struggling for year after year in the lower reaches of the Surrey staff at The Oval, and another Surrey batsman of the period, Roy Lewis, a name few will remember now although in 38 matches spread over six seasons between 1968 and 1973 he averaged 29 with the bat, better than – to take two players at random – 'Shrimp' Leveson-Gower and Harry Jupp, who both played for England in different eras. Lewis also had the same average exactly as Donald Knight, an England player of high class, and Alf Jeacocke, a fixture in the Surrey side for

many years. What made Lewis – and many others like him in many other counties that one could think of – different? The answer may be partly that it is a matter of luck and partly also that, in the old cliché, cricket is more than a game, more than a matter of runs and wickets. As in every profession a face must fit if it is to be accepted, and (again, always excepting the genius) things must be done in the 'right' way. I remember one batsman on the Surrey staff unleashing a splendid array of strokes in the last over before lunch and then being out l.b.w. to the last ball as he tried to sweep an off-spinner with his front foot a good way down the pitch. Arthur McIntyre's scorn for this display was made clearly apparent. He never became a regular county player and I doubt if it would have been different anywhere else.

Another illustration of the somewhat haphazard nature of the early days of a county cricketer was provided recently by Hugh Wilson, the tall young fast bowler who played several matches for Hampshire's Second XI and Club and Ground in the summer after he had left Wellington. Surrey spotted his potential, offered him terms, and he had just played his first Championship match for them, with some success, when he received a letter from Hampshire's coach offering him 'a game or two for the Second XI again this season'. Wilson got quite close to selection for the England tour of Australia in 1979–80 but spent most of 1980 back in the Surrey Second XI. Again, Paul Downton, who won his first England cap in Trinidad in 1981, had been a Second XI player for both Kent and Middlesex only a few months before.

The best job a young professional can land remains one on the Lord's Ground Staff, as Fred Titmus, Ian Botham and many others will confirm. Much of their life is menial in the extreme, with hours and days spent rolling pitches, selling scorecards, taking covers on and off the square and making up the numbers in M.C.C. sides of varying quality. But the members of the Lord's staff get a broad experience under wise guidance from old pros like Len Muncer and Harry Sharpe. It is said of Sharpe that he was approached one evening in the early summer of 1957 – just as he was clearing up the gear after a long and tiring day in the nets – by the fierce young fast bowler Roy Gilchrist, who was eager for his first bat of the tour. 'Me Roy Gilchrist', the conversation began. 'This ball. You bowl'. Sharpe's reply was as his name. 'Me Harry Sharpe. This ball. You f . . . off!'

C

ounty cricket is played by a circus of dedicated professionals watched by a small but equally dedicated band of supporters.

WOULD YOU HANG ON A MINUTE PLEASE?

A county cricketer's life has its drawbacks: little time is spent at home; it is physically demanding and mentally stressful since earning a good living depends more on personal performance than it does in most jobs; but very few of the 340-odd cricketers currently employed by the county clubs would swap their life of cameraderie in the open air for a nine-to-five job behind closed doors.

Frustrations exist, however, even in the best of jobs. In the days when the Pakistan Test cricketer Majid Khan was captaining Glamorgan, the team had to travel by coach one Saturday night all the way from Swansea to Buxton in Derbyshire

for a John Player League match the next day. Late at night the coach pulled up at the appointed inn. It was quite a small place and Mein Host looked rather aggrieved to hear a knock on his bolted front door.

'Who the bloody hell are you lot?' he inquired.

'Glamorgan'.

'Who?'

'Glamorgan County Cricket Club', continued the spokesman with unjustified confidence. 'We've booked here for the night'.

'I've got no bloody booking for Glamorgan County Cricket Club, and I'll tell you another thing Taff, I'm off to me flaming bed'.

Glamorgan had had a long day in the field and a long and back-aching drive afterwards. This was not good news at all. But captain Majid kept calm and ordered an immediate team meeting outside the nearby Buxton Bus Station. There he found inspiration in the form of some hard wooden benches. 'No problem', he said, with a peculiarly oriental calm and a few waggles of the head, 'we will sleep on benches.'

It was only because Tony Lewis had a friend at a country house nearby that the whole team did not, in fact, spend the night at the bus station. The following day Derbyshire beat Glamorgan – by one run.

A Yorkshire team had a similar experience when they turned up to fulfil a booking at a hotel which had been closed for three months. But on the whole today's county cricketer is comfortably

housed in good hotels and the bore of having to drive so many thousands of miles during the summer is offset by the fact that most of the travelling is done in cars donated or loaned free of charge by local garages.

More and more county cricketers are finding ways of spending their winters playing cricket overseas by taking coaching engagements with clubs in Australia, New Zealand or, more controversially, South Africa. It is a good way of spending the winter although it seldom works out that the player gets as much match practice as he is seeking. In Australia they play only one match a week, at the weekend; if it rains it is just bad luck. No wonder

Australian batsmen seldom throw their wickets away.

Many overseas players now make return visits in the British season although one Australian State player, engaged a few years ago to play a season for a Scottish League club, soon decided he had made a mistake. He was met at Glasgow Airport and told that there would be a reception for him at the club later that evening. It was suggested that he should have a shower and a rest before getting to the club at half-past seven. By half-past eight the officials and members were wondering what had happened to their new star player. Inquiries revealed that he had gone straight back to the airport, having booked an immediate

return flight from London to Perth in Western Australia!

The travelling life certainly does not suit everyone. In the Australian's case a sweetheart had been left behind and there is no doubt that the wives of county cricketers need to be long-suffering. Generally speaking, women do not like the irregular life-style and marriages are put under strain, frequently with fatal results for the relationship. It is not always so, of course, and to say that county cricketers have girls in every port would be to overstate the case, but cricket has its share of 'groupies' and the temptations are there. Such are the problems of the unsettled life, the irritations as well as the pleasures of travelling the country with the same small group of people, and the strains of having to succeed in order to hold down the job that, in the opinion of the former Oxford seam bowler, now clergyman, Andrew Wingfield-Digby, each side should have spiritual assistance in the form of a team chaplain!

For all the disadvantages, however, there are a greater number of plus factors, not the least being – for those who last the course, stay some ten years in the county team and put in the essential hard work in the relevant year – a tax-free benefit usually large enough to keep the cricketer and his family comfortably off for life. In the case of Jack Simmons, whose benefit with Lancashire in 1980 yielded £128,000, that is something of an understatement.

Moreover, there is the challenge of daily combat at a high standard, the satisfaction of success when things go right and a great mutual respect among players. Denis Compton was once beaten hopelessly in the air by the Gloucestershire off-spinner Tom Goddard but, as he fell over, stranded yards from his crease, he managed to late-cut the ball for four. 'One of these days', said Tom, 'there'll be no return ticket'. Years later he again beat Compton through the air and dismissed him. This time, with a bark of delight, he produced a single-fare bus ticket from his hip pocket!

It is a tough game, but generally also a chivalrous one. A young Nottinghamshire batsman, having been out for nought in the first innings of his first game in first-class cricket, faced Alex Skelding of Leicestershire in his second innings. His first ball, a lifter, brushed his glove and was caught by the wicket-keeper. Skelding began his triumphant instinctive appeal. He had got as far as 'Howz..' when he remembered it was the boy's first game and merely added to the umpire in a softer voice, '...yer father?'

The old pros can be hard on young players, too. Roger Knight, the present Surrey captain, remembers that as he was settling for his first ball in one of his earliest games for Cambridge, the Yorkshire captain Brian Close strolled across from short-leg and said: 'By the way, Sunshine, what's the Test score?' The young undergraduate's carefully built-up concentration was broken.

Close, of course, was tough enough himself. He deliberately let delivery after delivery from the ferocious Wes Hall hit him on the body at Lord's in 1963. On another occasion, when he was fielding at short-leg for Yorkshire, Martin Young of Gloucestershire was caught at slip from a rebound off the back of Close's famous bald head from a full-blooded pull off Fred Trueman. 'What would have happened if it had hit you straight in the temple?' Close was asked. The reply was typical, accompanied by a characteristic little laugh: 'He'd have been caught at cover instead'.

Another hardy perennial of the county circuit in an earlier age, Patsy Hendren, was also a man who used his experience to good effect. Alf Gover, the Surrey and England fast bowler, tells how he arrived, bursting with keenness, for his first match against Middlesex at Lord's.

WHICH WAY'S THE WICKET?

to bat, warmly greeted as usual by the crowd whose great favourite he was. Should he respect the old boy's wishes, or give him a bumper or two? County cricket is a tough game and Gover had a living to make: his competitive instincts won. His first ball was a bouncer. Hendren moved inside it with remarkably speedy reactions and hooked firmly for four. A lucky shot, thought Gover. His second bouncer went even more crisply against the fence in front of the Mound stand. The third went over that fence and amongst a cheering crowd.

It was a crestfallen Alf Gover who learned from Jack Hobbs at the end of the over that Patsy Hendren was not only one of the best hookers in the game still, but also, with his Irish blood, an incorrigible joker.

Humour is never far below the hard surface of county cricket. Sometimes it takes the form of the elaborate practical joke, such as the time when Peter Richardson 'set up' umpire Bill Copson to complain about the constant rumbling coming from the commentary box which was disturbing the batsmen's concentration. The victim was E. W. Swanton, booming away to his listeners in those well-known resonant tones and explaining that umpire Copson must be waving at somebody walking behind the bowler's arm. Colin Cowdrey, in on the joke, was summarizing in the box because of an injury and increased the commentator's embarrassment by cupping his hand and shouting back to Copson: 'Noise? What noise?'

'That rumbling noise in your commentary box', the umpire yelled back, to general amusement.

More often the humour is the apt off-the-cuff remark, such as the order given by the Middlesex captain John Warr as they came back to the dressing-room having been asked to follow-on after a collapse. 'Right boys', said Warr, 'same order, different batting'.

The best remarks often come in

Hendren was the only other man in the dressing-room when he arrived. 'What do you do, Son?' he asked, just to check the identity of the tearaway fast bowler he had heard about.

'I bowl', said Alf.
'Fast?'
'Very fast'.
'Listen', said Hendren confidentially. 'I'm getting on a bit, you know. Me peepers ain't what they was and the crowd 'ere like me to get a few. I don't mind how fast you bowl at me but don't give me any short stuff – I just can't see 'em any more'.

Cricket being what it is, it was inevitable that Gover should find himself bowling when Patsy Hendren waddled out adversity. The Kent players returned to the field at Canterbury after tea one day when they had been toiling in vain in the heat for many hours in ideal batting conditions. Derek Ufton noticed that, during the interval, a sleepy bee had alighted on the top of the stumps. 'What are we going to do with this?' he asked. 'Put it on a good length,' said Arthur Fagg, 'our bowlers will never disturb it there.'

Wicket-keepers are often as quick with the tongue as they are with their hands. It was Arthur Wood of Yorkshire who said to Hedley Verity, after that great spin bowler had been savaged for 30 runs in one over by the South African Jock Cameron: 'You've got him in two minds, Hedley. He doesn't know whether to hit you for four or six.'

There are a good many more overseas players in county cricket now than there used to be, and men of quite different colours and creeds play cheerfully together. Associations such as those between Zaheer Abbas of Pakistan and the South African Mike Procter for Gloucestershire, or Procter's compatriot Barry Richards and the Barbadian Gordon Greenidge for Hampshire, have made a nonsense of apartheid. Like the amateurs and professionals kept apart by convention in an earlier age, they learned that one man's hopes and fears are much like another's.

One man's temper, too, especially if he is a suffering bowler. George Macaulay once yelled in frustration at the Yorkshire slips, after yet another catch had gone to ground: 'I'd like to stuff the lot of you and put you all in Madame Tussaud's.'

'You can't do that until they're dead, George,' said mid-off in sympathetic response. 'And believe it or not I can still see their lips moving.'

Most women are attracted by cricketers rather than by cricket, if ever they are attracted to the game at all.

Yet, strangely enough, affection for a particular cricketer (which may or may not last!) often develops into affection for the game itself. The idea of a handsome athlete dressed all in white making graceful patterns with his body or his bat on the greensward is soon discovered to be as much a myth as that other ideal of cricket as a gentle and chivalrous game conducted ritually in the sunshine in beautiful surroundings. But the little mysteries of the game which gradually become apparent – cricket's slow drama and endless statistics – often grow on the female mind long after its owner has discovered that a man bowling with two silly short-legs is not a physical freak.

Girl-friends, wives, mothers or daughters...women so often have to put up with the obsession for cricket of their boy-friend, husband, son or father that many accept that if they cannot beat it, they might as well join in. Numerous players would be unable to flourish without the encouragement of women – although the old Yorkshire cricketer Ted Wainwright is supposed to have preferred to sleep with his bat!

The historical role of women in cricket is well known. In Surrey in 1778 Elizabeth Ann Burrell was reported to have 'got more notches in the first and second innings than any lady in the game', thus causing the Eighth Duke of Hamilton to fall in love with her. Christina Willes is credited with the development of round-arm bowling because, playing with her brother John in a barn in Kent, she found that under-arm bowling was impossible with a hooped skirt. Another famous round-arm bowler, William Lambert, also learned the art from a lady, his wife. And it was a group of women who burnt the bail which produced the Ashes in 1882–83.

Now the monstrous regiment is everywhere. They played a women's match between England and Australia at Lord's in 1976 to celebrate the Golden Jubilee of the Women's Cricket Association. There are women on county cricket club committees. B.B.C. Television employ a woman scorer. The daughter of the Indian Test batsman C. K. Nayudu commentates on cricket in India. Some women also umpire, others score and apart from the more traditional female roles of making teas, washing and ironing cricket shirts and consoling suicidal husbands when they have made a succession of ducks, a relatively small but certainly not insignificant number also *play*.

I have only once had the pleasure of playing in a properly organized match with women, for a scratch side against the England team at the Saffrons in Eastbourne. I remember the fast bowlers being relatively friendly, although the slow ones were subtle enough and when it came to batting I shall never forget Christine Whatmough of Kent hitting the ball as hard as almost any man.

The great publicist for women's cricket in recent times has been Rachael Heyhoe-Flint, captain of England for many years, a very good batsman and a very witty girl. She made one of the best impromptu remarks I have ever heard when presenting some new Gray Nicholls short-handled cricket bats to the members of the winning side after the first final of *The Cricketer* National Club Knockout at Edgbaston in

ESSEX CALAMITY

Even scorers need lavatories, and many keep theirs in a caravan which moves with them from ground to ground. At one time the Essex club used a former London bus, part of which was converted into a Ladies'. Once at Chelmsford a lady went in after close of play, and to her considerable alarm found herself being transported out of the ground and off to Westcliff for the following day's fixture.

1968. Ronnie Aird, then M.C.C. President, had presented the Derrick Robins Trophy and a cheque, and a director of the bat company was preparing to hand Rachael the bats one by one when he accidentally caught her in a very delicate abdominal region with one of the willows. She let out a loud squeal over the powerful loudspeakers and quickly defused any embarrassment by saying: 'Good thing it wasn't a *long* handle!'

Rachael Heyhoe-Flint is one of a line of lady cricketers who became famous names, at least in cricketing households. Myrtle Maclagen, Molly Hide, Betty Snowball, Mary Duggan and the Australian Betty Wilson were others, as was Enid Bakewell, the Nottinghamshire girl who produced brilliant feats in more recent times, interrupted only by occasional absences from the game to have children. Rachael herself offended a few but entertained many by pricking the

pomposity of some of the more serious and old-fashioned jolly-hockey-sticks types with whom serious women's cricket is still to a certain extent associated. Her favourite reply was to those who asked whether ladies, like men, find it necessary to protect their sensitive parts. 'Oh, yes', she would say, 'but we don't call them boxes, we call them man-hole covers'.

Despite all the publicity, men are sometimes unable to cope with the idea of women cricketers, not least the distinguished gentleman who during a speech at a mixed cricketing occasion referred to a former lady player present as being 'in my

COME ON ENID.
PUSH! OR
YOU'LL BE
STUMPED —

humble opinion one of the greatest hookers of her time.'

Some enlightened schools still offer cricket as a sport for girls as well as boys, but the number of specialist girls' schools playing the game has dwindled. They dropped cricket from the curriculum at Wycombe Abbey, the well-known Buckinghamshire school, at a time when I was depty editor of *The Cricketer*. Normally the magazine, even though it was then a fortnightly, had all too little space, but on

one occasion I found myself at the printer's with a small gap to fill on the letters page and nothing to fill it with. I therefore decided to impose upon the warm heart of my Aunt May, who had been a pupil there years before and in whose name I now wrote a strong letter, deploring the fact that the great game would no longer be played at Wycombe Abbey. Anyone reading the letter who had known my aunt as a schoolgirl must have been amazed. She had always loathed cricket and avoided playing it at all costs.

I

f you cannot play cricket for a living, perhaps the next best thing for addicts of the game is to try to write or speak about it.

The volume of letters I receive from young people aspiring to become cricket journalists is enough to underline my own good fortune. In fact I once wrote to Brian Johnston and asked how I could become a commentator. Like so many things, it is as much a question of luck and timing as anything else.

There can be little doubt that it is easier to write about cricket than it is to play it. On the other hand the job is open to similar pressures and short bursts of feverish activity at the end of long periods of concentrated effort. Most cricket writers are conscientious people and, like the players, find that the advantages of travel, not being tied to an office and doing an enjoyable job in convivial company are offset to some extent by the disadvantages of spending a great deal of time in cars or aeroplanes and long periods away from home. It is, without question, the perfect bachelor's life.

As in any job there are frustrations. E. W. 'Jim' Swanton has always believed that he failed to get the chance to cover the 'bodyline tour' of Australia in 1932–33 (which in the end was very inadequately covered in the Press, to say the least) because he had angered his sports editor by missing an edition one afternoon at Leyton when the only available telephone had been taken by another journalist. (The story was a good one: the record-breaking opening stand of 555 by Holmes and Sutcliffe.) In his later, *Daily Telegraph,* days Jim used to have a secretary to phone in his copy – a luxury rarely enjoyed by anyone else.

Overseas it can be a good deal harder than in England to get copy to the office on time. Some years ago, a writer on one of the popular papers eventually gave up using the inefficient telex system (nowadays it usually works well) during a match on a remote West Indian island and told his office he would instead use the telephone to phone his report through after the last day of the match, which was an important one just before a Test. However he had equal trouble getting through on the phone and only made contact, after three false alarms, at about half-past eleven at night, London time. As soon as he got through he said: 'Copy. Urgent', and waited anxiously to be transferred.

Some newspaper copytakers are notoriously uninterested in whatever it is they are obliged to take down.

'Who is it?' a weary voice eventually said.

The journalist gave his name, the topic and location, and added politely: 'Can you be as quick as you can, mate. It's urgent.'

'Hang on', said the copytaker, and there was a rustle of paper followed eventually by the rat-a-tat-tat of a typewriter. Then the bored-sounding voice spoke again: 'O.K. Go ahead.'

The writer had decided on a colourful start to his piece. It had been an outstanding win by M.C.C. on an island with Spanish historical associations. He therefore began dictating:

'Magnifico! Magnifico! This was an outstanding performance..'

'What?' said the voice in London. 'It's a bad line, you'll have to speak up.'

'Magnifico', repeated the writer.

'Eh?'

'Magnifico. M for Monkey, A for Apple, G for George, N for Nuts, I for Island, F for Freddie, I for Island, C for Charlie, O for Oswald.'

'Right', said the copytaker. 'Magnifico. I've got it. Carry on.'

'Magnifico!' said the writer, slightly hesitantly, a second time, only to get the irate retort:

'Alright, alright, I heard you the first time.'

Such frustrations are an occasional part of the job. On the whole, though, the Press-boxes of the cricket world are filled with characters prepared to put up with the occasional reverse and eager to enjoy the good times. Two inseparable companions during the summer months are Peter Laker of the *Mirror* and Basil Easterbrook of Thomson Newspapers. It was Basil who once phoned through his report on a League match in the North and, being somewhat pedantic at times, began by giving the copytaker his full name: 'Basil V. Easterbrook.' The reply was: 'Which League was that in?'

Small, rotund, bespectacled and a great gourmet, Basil reads novels at a faster rate than anyone I have ever met. Peter Laker is a great practical joker and spends much of his time trying to catch his friend out. During 1981 Easterbrook got his own back by pretending that he was going senile. Every now and then he would throw an irrational tantrum about the window being open too far or a strange smell which no-one else could detect; or he would pretend he had lost his hat when it was on his head; or suddenly begin a nonsensical sentence about a lady he knew in the High Street in Market Harborough. In the end no-one quite knew who was conning whom.

When he goes to Leeds, Peter Laker delights in putting anonymous calls through to the Sheffield cricket-writer Dick Williamson, a great stickler for cricket details, asking him some obscure question or other. He once rang Jack Fingleton and pretended to be a Monsieur Alphonse Dupont, a French cricket fanatic who had been Jack's lifelong admirer. Could he come up to the Press-box to meet him as he was visiting England? Jack went to some trouble to clear the way for his entry into the ground and into the box, and it took him a moment or two to realize who the very French-looking gentleman in a black beret really was.

Peter Laker is accident-prone. Among his many scrapes, he came close to being arrested on an aircraft in Pakistan when, soon after much publicity had been

SWANTON'S OUT OF ICE AGAIN.

given to a hijack in that part of the world, he walked onto the plane with two evil-looking daggers acquired somewhere near the North-West Frontier. His explanation that he was taking them home to his children in Sussex took some time to be believed and he was relieved of the weapons until he got to London. However, such is his capacity to survive that one has always felt there was a good chance of making it to the end of the journey if one was on the same plane as Peter. His special delight in Australia is taking dollars off the home journalists at pitch-and-toss. A former bowler on the Sussex staff, he is almost unbeatable, spinning the coin with uncanny precision, but the Australians can never resist a challenge or a gamble.

Cricket journalists, though Keith Fletcher used to know them collectively as 'the spies', seldom act in a body, tending rather to break up into various small cliques which, at least on tours, often see the 'popular' journalists in one group with the 'quality' men in another. The leaders of the latter group in recent years have been John Woodcock of *The Times* and Michael Melford of the *Daily Telegraph,* a modest though knowledgeable pair who prefer to spend such leisure hours as are possible on hectic modern tours at a golf club rather than on the beach or by the swimming pool. Many people in cricket journalism, myself included, owe much to the guidance of Jim Swanton, Melford's predecessor on the *Telegraph,* who used to do things in style wherever he went, never staying at a hotel if a Duke or a Maharajah was within range.

Jim Swanton used to travel Britain in the summer months with a secretary, and there tended to be a fairly swift turn-over because he was a stern taskmaster. One of his longest survivors was Daphne Surfleet, now Mrs Richie Benaud. Another, not quite so durable, was the former Richmond fly-half, Robin Whitcomb, who on one occasion took letters dictated by

Jim from his Jaguar as it was being lifted into the air on a garage ramp to have the tyres changed. When Jim was active as the Editorial Director of *The Cricketer* in its days in Great Portland Street, Robin used to go over to a pub called the Masons Arms on the other side of the road to get a gin and tonic at lunchtime each day, which he then carried back to the Master. One hot day the pub completely ran out of ice and Jim noticed at once when he was handed the glass that the ice was missing. Robin explained apologetically that the pub had completely run out. 'But,' said Jim, with a note of exasperation, 'didn't you tell them who the drink was *for?*'

In that same office of *The Cricketer* in 1967 I was clearing out the desk of Irving Rosenwater, my predecessor as Deputy Editor, a man of humble origins as well as a true fount of cricket knowledge. Amongst the scraps of paper in the desk drawers I came across a jar of a well-known brand of after-shave lotion. 'Is that Rosenwater's?' asked Jim. 'I presume it must be,' I said. Jim looked very perplexed and then said in a surprised voice: 'But that's the after-shave *I* use.'

Tony Pawson, the *Observer* cricket-writer who also did the Deputy Editor's job for a while, tells how he was rung up by Jim at the printer's and told that he must include a last minute review of the latest volume of *Wisden*. Tony protested that it was very late in the printing process and that in any case the printers were going slow. It was too late to commission a special article. Jim insisted so Tony said that the only answer would be for him to write the review himself at the printer's. 'Oh, alright,' said Jim after an exasperated grunt. 'But you must remember that with us the review of *Wisden* is normally the occasion for some *good* writing.'

Jim's own outstanding contributions to cricket literature are well enough known and I tell these tales of a larger-than-life character with affection and gratitude for the help and encouragement he has given me. One last memory of our association on *The Cricketer*: Jim used to commission articles from far and wide and was never refused owing to his own, and the magazine's, prestige, despite the fact that the payment was (in those days) somewhat paltry. Jim had a regular phrase when writing to well-known authors: '...even to the great and famous our fee cannot exceed a guinea per 100 words.' One day he got a letter back from J. J. Warr which went like this:
'Dear Jim,
I shall be delighted to do the 1,000 word piece you asked for. If I may say so, your rate of a guinea a word is more than generous.
Yours ever,
J. J.'
It is a pity John Warr did not remain a cricket journalist for longer than he did, for he is a noted wit who once said of the medium-paced New Zealand Test bowler Bob Cunis that 'his bowling, like his name, is neither one thing nor the other.'

There are plenty of characters amongst the cricket-writers of other countries too, and the cameraderie of the game extends to the Press-box with warm personalities like Mike Coward from Adelaide and Brian Mossop from Melbourne keeping the atmosphere jovial

AND CHRIS. DID YOU ASK HIM ABOUT THE AFFAIR HIS WIFE IS HAVING WITH .... ?

C.M.J.

in Australia, where Press facilities are often as inadequate as they are on many grounds in England when it comes to watching the game in any comfort or from a suitable position. Mossop works on the *Sydney Morning Herald,* in conjunction with the great Bill O'Reilly, a man who speaks his mind with unimpeachable authority. At times he can strike one as a little stern (he was for some years a schoolmaster) but he is not a man with any bitterness in him, unlike another well-known Australian cricket-writer who, in 1974–75, walked round the vast Melbourne Cricket Ground with me at the end of a game to catch the coach which was to take teams and Press to the airport.

After a long walk round the concrete perimeter of the ground (it was hot and humid and it had been a hard day's work) we were appalled to find the gate behind which the coach was parked locked and barred. The time for the coach's departure was imminent but there was nothing for it but to walk all the way round to the main gate on the other side of the ground. It was nobody's fault and, knowing the customary Australian friendliness, I was somewhat disillusioned by the reaction of my colonial cousin. He spat twice and said through clenched teeth: 'Fancy following a f...... Pom!'

Test cricket has always been the apogee of the game, which is why the rival World Series games under Mr Packer's auspices in Australia were called 'Super-Tests' and were such a threat to the real thing.

WHAT TIME'S TEA DEAR? THE BOYS NEED THE PRACTICE —

What they lacked was certainly not quality of cricket, or, from the players' point of view, a sense of true competitiveness. Those who played in W.S.C. all say it was at least as tough as Test cricket. But the games did lack, from the cricket follower's viewpoint, the sense of national involvement which makes Test cricket such a life-or-death business: if you like, a substitute for war.

Once upon a time Test cricket was not necessarily the supreme trial of strength. H.K. Foster, probably the second best of the seven brothers of a Malvern clergyman who all played for Worcestershire (they used to throw the plates to one another when washing up in the kitchen), said that he had no wish to play for England. Another great early amateur, Reggie Spooner, turned down the chance to captain England in Australia for business reasons, something that would be unthinkable for a young cricketer today. There were, as a result, some distinctly fortunate additions to the hallowed ranks of Test cricketers, amongst them the Irishman J. E. P. McMaster, who went in number nine for England in a Test in Cape Town in 1888–89, scored nought in both innings and neither bowled nor took a catch. For Australia Roland Pope, effectively the team doctor, found himself playing a Test in Melbourne when several players dropped out because of a disagreement over pay. What is more, having made a duck in the first innings, he actually scored three in the second! Indeed he did better than Roy Park whose wife bent down to pick up her knitting just as he was about to face his first ball against England at Melbourne in 1920–21 and thereby missed seeing his entire Test batting career!

(Perhaps it was some consolation that his nephew, Ian Johnson, later went on to captain Australia.)

Nowadays cricketers do not become Test players by accident, although the journalist and former Cambridge Blue Henry Blofeld nearly made a 'dream' appearance in India in 1964 when so many players were ill that England only just found eleven fit men. There are more Test players today because there are many more Tests, so much so that the players, frequently televised, are becoming too familiar, losing their mystique, and the matches themselves are losing their sense of occasion. Between September 1979 and February 1980, for example, Australia alone played 22 Test matches against five different opponents: there *are* only five opponents for them to play in any case until such time as South Africa abandons apartheid or Sri Lanka is admitted to the élite.

Along with a Test cap there now comes not only fame but fortune. The basic pay for an England player in a home Test of £1,400 a match is supplemented by substantial win bonuses, additional prize money, a possible share of 'man of the match' and 'man of the series' awards and a a cut of the various commercial deals now being laid on for Test teams by companies like Mark MacCormack's organization

A DUBIOUS BENEFIT

J.E. Shilton, the Warwickshire left-arm bowler, had the misfortune to be arrested for debt in 1895 only days before his benefit match. He was saved at the eleventh hour by the county club agreeing to pay the money into Court. The match, against Yorkshire, went ahead, and Shilton to his relief was released from prison, played, and collected his benefit – though minus the amount already paid out by the club.

which makes so much for tennis and golf stars. No wonder players say it's not the game it was!

It is not necessarily easy money, however. A Test lasts a week if you take into consideration the gathering of the team for nets on the day before the match and the rest day which still exists for the majority of Tests. In that time the player is under severe public scrutiny and failure must be very painful. To enter a dressing-room during a Test is to discover a new level of intensity in cricket. Amongst all the jumble of bats, pads, gloves, helmets, boots, medical apparatus and towels the most important item of equipment seems to be chewing gum, vigorously munched by most of the players to soothe their nerves and tighten their concentration.

Nerves can upset the staunchest of characters. One day in Australia in the 1920s Maurice Tate was appalled to find that his boots had disappeared before a day in the field. The England players turned the dressing-room upside-down in vain but Tate had to bowl in borrowed boots which fitted his enormous feet badly. He returned to the dressing-room at the end of the day in agony, with his toes all skinned. Delving miserably into his bag for some plasters he found his boots, hidden in an old pair of flannels. On such chances Tests have been won or lost.

Frank Hayes, the Lancashire batsman who scored a hundred in his first Test against the West Indies in 1973, was so nervous before going in to bat during the tour of the Caribbean early in 1974 that he was more than once physically sick before a Test innings.

David Steele, the grey-haired, bespectacled hero of England's fights against Thomson and Lillee in 1975, had an inauspicious start to the first of his many defiant innings for his country. Picked, to general surprise, to go in at number three, he was soon called into action when Barry Wood was out l.b.w. to Dennis Lillee.

With the good wishes of his colleagues still in his ears, Steele went downstairs from the England dressing-room (on the right of the Lord's Pavilion as you look out) and a few moments later found himself not in the Long Room, where he should have been, but in the Gentlemen's lavatory in the basement. In the consternation of the moment he had gone down two flights of stairs instead of one. Wood had already passed through the Long Room when Steele appeared, to Wood's surprise, going upstairs instead of down. 'Where are you going? Get a move on', Wood said. Steele coolly asked what the ball was doing, then made his way through the crowded Long Room towards the steps leading down past the members to the green outfield below. Just as he reached the first of the steps he heard one man say: 'Bloody hell, he's a bit grey isn't he?'

Steele looked like a village cricketer but played like a hero in a Test against Australia at Lord's. That is the original and the ultimate cricketing dream come true.

Steele presumably suffered from the right kind of nerves: he was tense enough to be on edge, with his senses at their sharpest, but not so wound up that he froze. I remember Mike Brearley telling me that his legs felt like jelly when he walked out for his first Test innings at Trent Bridge and Alan Jones, the Glamorgan batsman whose record in county cricket suggests he should have played plenty of Test cricket, was unable to do himself any justice through sheer shaking when he played his only representative game for England against the Rest of the World.

The late Ken Barrington also used to get very keyed up before a Test innings, chain-smoking often before he went out to bat, but in his case his intense pre-occupation with the job in hand always had the right effect when he got to the crease. His concentration, discipline and courage are legendary and the word grim often comes to mind in connection with the batting of a man who in fact had a tremendous sense of fun.

Test cricket, if not always grim, has certainly always been tough ever since the days when Ernie Jones sent a bouncer whistling through W. G's beard. ('What's all this Jonah?' 'Sorry, Doctor, she slipped.' There would be no apologies nowadays.) Since the introduction of prize-money the sense of 'needle' has become ever sharper: the umpire often suffers most but Arthur Fagg once got his own back on Bill Lawry when he had given him out, much to the Australian captain's obvious displeasure. 'How the hell could that have been out?' Lawry whined as he walked past Fagg. 'L.b.w.', said Fagg. 'How could it have been l.b.w., I hit the bloomin' ball', replied Lawry. 'Yes, I know, that's why I gave you out caught behind!'

Many players believe it is easier playing Test cricket away from home, not least because, on many tours, a real esprit de corps builds up. It is not so easily achieved at home when a side gathers only on the day before the Test and breaks up again six days later. It is on tours that the character of cricketers becomes even more important. Ken Barrington was perhaps the ideal 'tourist'. Meticulous about all he did he would never lose a suitcase or appear late for a journey. He would practise diligently. He would play every innings as if the future of his country depended on his own performance. Not least, he would keep the morale of his colleagues high with his bubbling enthusiasm, quick wit and his gift of mimicry. Amongst his favourites were Alf Gover, who speaks in a deep-voiced mumble punctuated by 'Old Boy', and, more recently, Graham Gooch. It used to hurt Ken that Gooch, in his earlier Test days, used to seem so untroubled by getting out, and on the Australian tour he would imitate the big amiable Essex batsman coming back into the dressing-room, giving a brief and laconic description of his dismissal, then getting on his sun-glasses and going out to sunbathe!

Tours bring out the best and the worst in cricketers, on and off the field. As a player Barrington used to love the slow, true wickets of India, matching the oriental patience with his own blend of grit, discipline and determination. It was on one of his earlier tours that he asked a waiter for a coconut and was served with a coca cola and a plate of nuts; and on another that he was asked for his autograph by a small boy, found that the pen he had been handed was not working and then had his clean whites and touring blazer covered in ink as the youth shook the pen in front of him! It was also in India that he had some back trouble and asked for a harder bed to be delivered to his room. The mattress was removed and a hard wooden board inserted under the sheets instead. Unknown to him, however, the bed being used by Barrington's room-mate Peter Parfitt had also been 'improved' in this way. Parfitt came chirpily into the room after a long day in the field, and threw himself bottom-first onto his 'mattress' only to end up with even more severe back trouble than his colleague!

As a manager Ken was prone to the occasional endearing Spoonerism. He told an intense gathering of cricket administrators in Sri Lanka: 'I can promise you, gentlemen, you haven't fallen down on any failings'. He described Geoff Boycott's batting as being 'second to anyone's in the world', and an innings of Tony Greig's as being a 'great performance in anyone's cup of tea'. On a more recent tour of Australia he reported that he had been to see a Yugoslav football team the previous evening called 'Red Star Belgravia'.

There was another side to Ken's humour. He enjoyed making people laugh, and on tours this could do wonders for morale. Coming down to breakfast one day at our comfortable hotel near King's Cross in Sydney, he mentioned that he had tried one of the alka-seltzer tablets which the management thoughtfully left in each bathroom. 'I tell you what, though', he said, 'they don't half make your mouth froth'.

Australian Tests in recent years have increasingly taken on the overtones of show-business. During the lunch interval some additional entertainment, ranging from athletics races to pop concerts, are provided for the crowd and for a time there was a fashion for a sky-diver to appear at the start of each Test, bringing with him the coin which the two captains were to toss for innings. John Woodcock suggested that *Wisden* would soon be recording not just the names of the teams and the umpires but the sky-divers as well!

The toss before a Test in India has its own drama. Both there and in the West Indies the crowd often seem to sense if the home captain has won the toss even before the coin has landed. One Indian captain in opposition to the great Sir Garfield Sobers is alleged to have said 'We'll bat' after Sobers had correctly called 'Heads'. This captain had been a hero with the home crowd and dared not fail.

Certainly the sheer volume and passion of crowds in India is unmatched, although opinions among players vary over which is the most daunting audience to play before: that at Calcutta, where the ground once called Eden Gardens is now a vast concrete amphitheatre, or at Melbourne, where the emotive initials M.C.G. in 1960–61 during the famous of great sporting deeds before enormous crowds. Some 90,800 spectators attended the second day of the Fifth Test at the M.C.G. in 1960–61 during the famous 'Worrell v. Benaud' series. On these occasions some players are plainly terrified, others are inspired. Tony Greig was the classic example in recent years of someone who played better the bigger the crowd and the occasion: a natural showman, he yet conrived to be detached from the bedlam around him, able to keep cool and concentrate.

The ability to give of his best in a crisis, or in a hostile atmosphere, or when handicapped by illness, as Greig was during his match-winning hundred at Calcutta in 1976–77, is often what separates Test cricketers of equal ability. Sometimes, of course, illness wins. Ian Peebles left the most graphic example in his description of Alf Gover running in to bowl shortly after rising from his sickbed to play a match in India for Lionel Tennyson's touring team:

'During his third over only the most acute observer would have been alarmed at the tense expression on his face as he started on his long, hustling run. It was when he shot past the crouching umpire and thundered down the pitch with the undelivered ball in his hand that it became obvious that something was amiss. The batsman, fearing a personal assault, sprang smartly backward, but the flannelled giant sped past looking to neither right nor left. Past wicket-keeper, slips and fine-leg in a flash, he hurtled up to the pavilion steps in a cloud of dusty gravel and was gone'.

. . . and for a time there was a fashion for a sky-diver to appear at the start of each Test, bringing with him the coin which the two captains were to toss for innings.

HEADS

A sense of humour is the other great ally to a touring cricketer. That jovial Geordie heavyweight Colin Milburn, whose career was so tragically cut short when he lost the sight of his left eye in a car accident, had been playing with great success for Western Australia in the Sheffield Shield when he was summoned to join the M.C.C. side in Pakistan in 1969. Milburn's cheerful presence immediately lifted the spirits of his colleagues. Indeed, to show their appreciation of his flying to join them in order to play in the final Test of the series, the whole team went along to the airport at Dacca and garlanded him with flowers, to the amazement of airport officials. He then solemnly shook hands with each player. The team was staying at by far the best hotel in Dacca, a modern and comfortable one, but in a prearranged hoax Milburn was taken by coach to the seediest old guest-house they had been able to locate. Colin Cowdrey took his new arrival in to sign the register and only burst out laughing when Milburn, with a look of horror on his face as he put down his heavy bags in the fly-ridden, pokey, old-fashioned corridor which served as the 'foyer,' said: 'Bloody Hell! All the way from Australia to stay in a dump like this.'

The journey may have been worth it for, in what was to be his last Test innings, Milburn scored a brilliant hundred off 163 balls. It was his only innings in Pakistan and the match ended a day early because of a particularly violent riot.

It is well known that West Indian crowds have a tendency to get over-excited at times. During a riot in one Test the B.B.C. commentator Rex Alston is reputed to have said with great emphasis: 'This is disgraceful; they are behaving like animals down there.' He forgot, unfortunately, that even in a riot some spectators were sticking to the West Indian habit of keeping their transistor radios close to their ears throughout the match. Within seconds the commentators were ducking below the windows of the commentary-box as the bottles and stones came flying in a new direction.

Peter May delights in telling how, during the riot on his tour of the Caribbean in 1960, a very efficient squad of police quickly arrived on the scene, each with a long hose pipe. They fanned out to confront the offenders and waited for the commanding officer to drop his arm to signal the water to be released in a mighty jet. Alas, nothing happened. One of the crowd had nipped round behind the pavilion and cut off the water supply!

Of all the human elements in cricket, none is more important to a good game than a decent pair of umpires.

REMEMBER PLINK.
MARTIN-JENKINS TAKES
A DIVE IN THE
SECOND OVER!

It was the Australian player Sid Barnes who picked up a dog during a Test match, ran with it to the wicket and presented it to the umpire saying: 'Here you are, all you need now is a white stick.' All that umpires really need is good eyesight and hearing, a knowledge of the laws and impartiality. An alarming number of umpires, however, lack at least one of those virtues, if not all three.

I was once talking to a first-class umpire at a huge reception in the State Government buildings opposite the Windsor Hotel in Melbourne when he made an unfortunate slip of the tongue. 'My ambition', he told me, 'is to umpire for Australia.'

In fact, at the highest level it is very rare indeed to see umpiring which is obviously not strictly impartial, although a cynical English journalist used to say whenever he saw the umpires coming out to start a session of play in a certain part of the world: 'Ah well, better sit down and get settled again; here comes the cheats.' It is well known, of course, that all visiting cricket teams believe at some point of their tour that they have been the victim of home-town decisions, hence the recent calls, with prize-money now substantial, to have neutral umpires for Test series.

It is at club and village level, however, that umpires really can be an important member of the side. I shall never forget a match, in the days before twenty overs in the last hour became compulsory by law, when the visiting umpire shamelessly walked off five minutes early when the side I was playing for were within a few runs of victory. Our own umpire looked surprised when his colleague lifted off the bails and walked in, but said nothing: in these circumstances the stronger character wins and umpires who do the job regularly tend to act as a pair and defend each other against a hostile world.

The cry of 'Owzat, Father?' and the response, 'Owt, Son' is familiar in English

folk-lore, but I know of at least one village club where both question and answer were frequently heard until the son became too old to bowl. His ancient father still dons the white coat from time to time.

At another village club I know, not far away in the same county of Surrey, the regular umpire was a very loquacious little man who each weekend used to claim a record for the number of games in which he had stood. As you were backing up when batting he would whisper out of the side of his mouth: 'It's me four thousand, four hundred and forty-ninth game today, y'know.' He finally had to give up after a particularly unfortunate match. First he forgot himself at a moment of tension by letting out a loud appeal for a catch behind the wicket when he was standing at square-leg. Then, later in the same game, he signalled four with his usual flourish when a ball had reached the boundary and an instant later called out, in a stentorian voice: 'Scorer! One short!'

Such men need to be humoured. Understanding an umpire and getting him on your side, either as batsman or bowler, is as important an art as batting or bowling itself. After all, your success depends to a certain extent upon the decisions of the man in the white coat. You have to get to

know the breed. All are impressionable, even if few are actually corruptible. The least you can be is polite. Most umpires like a bit of chat, either in the field or, especially, at the crease. You should start with the weather, or the state of the match, then graduate to more personal matters. A little flattery helps: 'You must be very experienced at this game', or 'That was a very good decision just then, if I may say so'. Sometimes more direct methods are needed. 'This chap will never get an l.b.w. unless he goes round the wicket, will he?' or 'I don't blame you for not calling no-ball every time he lands his front foot over the crease because it's not properly marked, is it?' When it is your turn to bowl, you may just need to make a couple of speculative appeals before venting the utterly convincing one when an l.b.w. or a caught-behind really *does* seem out.

The art of the convincing appeal has never been more effectively demonstrated than it is in first-class cricket these days, and although gamesmanship may rightly be deplored there is nothing new about it. The stories of W.G.'s expertise in this field are well known and if even half of them are true he was clearly a man who in modern terminology would be called competitive. He once ran out a batsman who was doing some innocent 'gardening' in mid-pitch and is reputed to have been fond, when bowling, of pointing to a passing flock of birds in the path of the sun in order to dazzle the batsman! Sometimes the umpire got the better of him. 'The wind's deuced strong today, umpire', he once said after being bowled by a ball that just clipped his bails. As he bent to replace them and carry on batting he heard the reply: 'Yes, Doctor. Hope it won't blow your hat off on the way back to the pavilion.' On another occasion he disliked the decision given against him so much that he squeaked: 'Shan't have it, can't have it, *won't* have it'. To which the reply from Surrey's Walter Read was: 'But you'll

have to have it, Doctor.'

Obstinacy is a characteristic common to almost all umpires, who come in a variety of shapes, sizes and types, although the majority of regulars are elderly and tend to be small of stature. Umpires who sit on shooting-sticks, those who talk a great deal, and those who are either very young and officious or very old and casual are the most dangerous. All these types are frequently found in amateur cricket, although *any* umpire who enjoys his hobby and takes it fairly seriously is probably better than none at all because this means that members of the batting side perforce take on the job themselves and, as all umpires know, players *never* know the laws.

In English first-class cricket, of course, nearly all the umpires have played the game to a high standard. In Australia it is not always so; witness the Test umpire Peter Cronin who never played more than a few school games but devoted himself to learning the umpiring art. In county cricket, however, it is undoubtedly a help both to umpires and to players that the officials should have played the game and so thoroughly understand its pressures and problems. This gives them an authority that once they did not have. It is no longer thinkable, for example, that anyone should get away with what Harry Jupp, the Dorking favourite, did in about 1870 when he was castled by the first ball of the match. Like W.G. he replaced the bails at once, whereupon the somewhat timid umpire inquired: 'Ain't you going, Juppy?' 'No', was the stolid reply, 'not at Dorking I ain't'. And he did not.

The modern first-class umpire is held in greater respect, though none of the present day has quite the same aura of authority that Frank Chester or Syd Buller possessed. Many Australian umpires have the same air of command – Col Egar, Mel McInnes and Tom Brooks were perhaps the best of recent times. Brooks was a determined guardian of batsmen, generally speaking, when he considered they were unable to protect themselves against too many bumpers, although those who played with Tom himself say that he hurled a good many short ones around batsmen's ears in his time. Perhaps hypocrisy is another essential characteristic of all players-turned-umpires who, after all, are only poachers transformed into gamekeepers!

John Snow, England's self-styled 'rebel' fast bowler, said during a famous court case that he once had nightmares about having nothing better to do than to become a first-class umpire when he retired from playing. Yet Snow had the stubborn streak which would have made him an excellent official in a white coat. He and the Brisbane policeman Lou Rowan used to clash like rutting stags in the Highlands in spring, with the watching public in the role of the female deer. Neither would be seen to allow his manhood to be undermined. It seemed at times in the 1970–71 series in Australia that the batsman was an irrelevance and that the real duel was between umpire and fast bowler! Snow was a very good man to have on any side, both gifted and determined, but he would be the first to admit that bowing to authority was not his strongest point. Once rather pompously told that he was a 'very stupid young man', he replied to the distinguished cricketing personality who had delivered this cutting verdict: 'Maybe. But you are a very stupid *old* man.'

Repartee of a slightly less sharp kind has been the stock-in-trade of some of the best-loved umpires. Alex Skelding's catch-phrase at the end of the day as he took off the bails – 'That concludes the entertainment for the day, gentlemen' – was as famous as any comedian's and Bill Reeves's reply to R.W.V. Robins has become equally celebrated. Robins, having had an appeal or two turned down during an unlucky over with his leg-breaks, was asked by Reeves if he would like his Middlesex sweater, complete with its three dangerous-looking seaxes. Robins, always liable to be somewhat fiery, told the umpire where he could put the sweater. 'What, Mr Robins', said Reeves in mock surprise, 'swords and all?'

On another occasion Reeves gave out the young Denis Compton rather dubiously, when he had made only 14, to end the Middlesex innings. Gubby Allen, the non-striker, suggested politely that it had been a pretty rough decision. 'True', said Bill, 'but he's good enough to get a hell of a lot of runs in the years ahead, and I'm dying for a pee.'

Unfortunately it isn't nowadays so easy for umpires to be light of heart. They used to be, like *Times* correspondents, anonymous figures, seldom even mentioned on the scorecards in the newspapers. Now television has made Test umpires public figures and they are paid accordingly. But much calumny awaits them if their split-second decisions are considered wrong. They cannot heed the advice of James J. Boren, founder of the International Association of Professional Bureaucrats: 'If in doubt mumble, if in trouble delegate, if in charge ponder.' Umpires, poor chaps, can only ponder for so long and nothing will alter the time-honoured advice to all cricketers: if at first you don't succeed, blame it on the umpire.

The first cricket commentary, in the broad sense of the word, to be broadcast on sound radio was made by Sir Pelham (then still P.F. or 'Plum') Warner.

It was a direct report from Leyton on the Essex versus New Zealanders match of 1927. The next was made by Canon F.H. Gillingham, the Essex batsman, from the Oval; when obliged to 'fill in' for a break between the innings, he unfortunately offended B.B.C. principles by describing in some detail the various advertisements around the ground. In these commercially minded days one would be able to go through the whole of a lunch interval using that method, but mention of any product or firm other than the match sponsors is still, of course, taboo.

The first Test match to be covered in any depth by the B.B.C. was the Oval Test of 1930 when John Snagge acted as presenter and 'stand-by' to the South African Test player Aubrey Faulkner. Eight years later the Second Test at Lord's became the first cricket match ever televised, and H.B.T. 'Teddy' Wakelam was the commentator. While Howard Marshall was doing the radio commentary, setting in his mellifluous voice the style which is still very much followed today, Wakelam was back on television later that summer (his audience, presumably, being far smaller than Marshall's) recording the course of Len Hutton's immortal 364 at The Oval.

These were still very much pioneering days, of course, and at the end of the match at The Oval Wakelam interviewed several members of the crowd. The idea was to talk about the match but one old man with a beard looked straight at the camera and said that he was delighted to have the opportunity to tell a wide audience about his revolutionary new calendar. Apparently he was still expanding on his theme twenty minutes later, unaware that the camera had ceased functioning, and that his voice had stopped broadcasting nineteen minutes earlier.

Usually it is the cricket broadcaster himself who suffers moments when he wishes he had been taken off the air. I doubt if the feeling ever came to Jim Swanton, another of the pioneers, who broadcast the first hat-trick during the first regularly broadcast overseas tour (M.C.C. in South Africa in 1938–39) or to the incomparable John Arlott, who must have won more listeners to cricket than anyone and who was never at a loss for an apt comment. When, for example, 'Tufty' Mann of South Africa bowled George Mann of England he at once referred to 'Mann's inhumanity to Mann'.

The apt phrase and vivid description rolled from John's measured voice like silk handkerchiefs from a conjuror's pocket: 'Lindwall turns in a

COULD DO BETTER

A strong candidate for poorest county batting performance must be that of G. Deyes (Yorkshire) in 1907. In his first 14 innings he scored 0, 0, 0,* 1, 1,* 0, 0, 0, 0, 1,* 0, 0, 0, 0. Towards the end of the season he improved, hitting 4, 1 and 12 in his last three visits to the wicket. This last flurry gave him a final average of:
Inns 17 N.o. 3 Runs 20
Highest score 12 Average 1.42.

smooth arc, his shirt fills with wind, and he moves in now on that easy, low-slung approach, gradually gathering pace...' 'Hendrick, broad-shouldered, deep-chested, slim about the hips, mops his brow briefly and prepares to bowl again to Richards...' 'Edrich played at that one, missed it, and looked up at Hall like a small boy caught stealing jam.' Arlott never made the listener blush.

Some commentators, however, are accident-prone, and in the case of Brian Johnston, one might guess almost deliberately so, because the more laughs a match provides him, the happier he is (and his devoted listeners too). I have only once heard him totally speechless and, perhaps fortunately, it was when *Test Match Special* was only being broadcast on the World Service. It was during a very unlikely match between England and Canada at Old Trafford in the 1979 Prudential World Cup. One of the Canadians left the field and was replaced by one of their reserve players. Knowing Brian is not very good at pronouncing long or unusual names and that he had no idea who the substitute fielder was, I pointed on the scorecard to the name of a player called Showkat Bash. For the next few seconds Brian shuddered with uncontrollable giggles which were so contagious that no-one else in the commentary-box could speak either.

It was a case of the biter bit, for Brian is always playing jokes of his own. On one occasion during a Trent Bridge Test he noticed the Australian commentator Alan McGilvray taking a large mouthful of cake at the back of the box and promptly asked him to come to the microphone to give the latest news from the dressing-room of one of the Australian players who had been injured. Alan is a perfectionist who rightly takes his job very seriously, and he was highly embarrassed when bits of cake flew in all directions from his mouth as he tried to reply, until Brian explained what had happened and all of us, Alan

included, could laugh about it!

Brian was himself the victim of another joke when he was broadcasting for B.B.C. Television one of the Sunday afternoon Rothman's Cavaliers matches which were the forerunners of the John Player League. He had to interview various people including, on this occasion, the Indian captain Ajit Wadekar as he came back to the pavilion after being dismissed. 'Bad luck, Wadders,' said B.J. in his normal breezy manner to a man he knew quite well. 'That looked a good delivery, did it move a bit?' Wadekar looked blank and Brian repeated the question. Again no response. At the third attempt Wadekar (who had been put up to the leg-pull in advance by the Nawab of Pataudi) said: 'Sorry, no speak English,' and disappeared up the pavilion steps leaving an embarrassed Johnston in his wake!

Over the years, indeed, Brian has had some trouble with Indian cricketers. In 1952 he interviewed the Indian team manager Mr P. Gupta and got on to the subject of the team for the next Test. 'By the way,' said Brian, 'are you a selector?' 'No,' replied the manager, 'I'm a Christian.'

There have been only a few occasions when I have come near to changing my conviction that to be a cricket broadcaster is the ideal occupation. The most recent was in March 1981 when I heard a smooth, slow Radio Three voice say: 'Now it is time for *Test Match Special*, introduced by Christopher Martin-Jenkins.' The snag was that I was listening not in a studio, ready for action, but in the middle of a creeping mass of cars and lorries inching their way up Knightsbridge. Quite why my reaction should have been Germanic I don't know but all I could do was to grip the steering wheel still more tightly and roar at the top of my voice and from the depths of my being: 'GOTT IN HIMMEL!' A cyclist overtaking me to my right nearly fell off in his surprise, even though my windows were shut against the traffic rumble; and a lady in a Morris 1100 on my left looked at first shocked and then embarrassed, as though she would rather not be seen in the same traffic jam as an obvious lunatic.

What made it worse was that I had failed even to let my producer, Peter Baxter, know that I was not going to make it on time. Telephone booths had been occupied all the way through Putney and Fulham and when, to my relief, I finally found two together the first, after a woman had taken an age to gather up her belongings into her bag having made her call, refused to give any dialling tone. The one next door also refused for a time, then mercifully did so. With about five minutes to go to transmission I at last heard the phone ringing the B.B.C. number. I had three ten pence pieces, but all the machine did was to swallow them gratefully and come back each time with a merry pip-pip-pip. I was powerless.

Back in the car I waited for that announcement in artificial calm. They like to have long pauses on Radio Three and it seemed more like minutes than seconds before a slightly breathless Peter Baxter said: 'Well, not Christopher Martin-Jenkins actually. I think he may be stuck in a traffic jam somewhere in London . . .'

My mind went back to one of the first broadcasts I had made, which was a football 'round-up' contribution to the *Sports Report* programme made famous by Angus Mackay and Eamonn Andrews.

Most of the studios in Broadcasting House are in the basement. The Sports Room is on the third floor. The football results start to come in at about ten to five over the teleprinters and details of the second halves of the sixty-odd matches come pouring in like water at about the same time. On this occasion I had managed, despite a sort of cold creeping panic, to wade through at least some of the sea of news tape, and in a shaking hand to write out at least a part of the main news, onto numerous sheets of rustly white paper.

All the time other more experienced members of the Sports staff were trying to help me with such comments as: 'Are you all right, Chris? You're sure you're O.K.? Don't worry, you've got at least another minute before you're on the air. Did you see that Bremner was sent off? Gosh, did you see this? Hately got a hat-trick. You *must* give this, Chris! Don Revie had an argument with the ref. at Elland Road. Quick, Chris, you'd better get down to the studio, it's 5.15.'

So, my mind in whirl, desperately trying to remember if it was Hately who had been sent off and Bremner who had got a hat-trick, or vice-versa, I rushed, heart beating like a hammer, to the lifts.

I pushed the right button several times. But though the lifts kept on coming *up*, not one of them seemed to want to go down. Eventually there came a polite inquiry from the *Sports Report* producer. It went something like this: 'I wonder where that new fellow is, he seems to be a little late.' It might conceivably have been worded a bit more strongly.

At any rate I was advised to forget the lift and to sprint back so that I could do the broadcast from the makeshift studio in the Sports Room above. This I attempted to do into a lip mike – the first time I had used one. The snag with a lip-mike is that, to a novice, both ends of it look much the same. Unfortunately I chose the *wrong* one.

My opening words were therefore lost to the world, until a sweaty hand from behind pulled the mike out of my hand, another one clasped me firmly across the mouth, and a third turned the microphone round the correct way, and thrust it back into my own shaking paw. Then, with a desperate gasp for breath, I was finally off on my stumbling way.

Not too long after this, I was entrusted with the introduction of my first Saturday half-hour programme, the one

I'LL HAVE TO GO NOW, DORIS. — I THINK SOMEONE'S WAITING TO USE THE PHONE....

which used to go out at half-past six, entitled *Sports Session*. Everything went very happily until the final five minutes of the programme. All that my script instructed me to do in this period was to introduce the rugby results, then read the racing results, then close the programme. Unfortunately, the man reading the rugby results was another green performer who, in his youth, had suffered from a stammer. His effort on this occasion was little short of disastrous. Not only did his stutter return with a vengeance, but the pages of his script got stuck together and he lost his place. Eventually, after about a minute of increasingly incoherent jabberings, he dried up altogether. There was a horrible pause of fifteen seconds or so – again, they seemed like minutes – as he struggled desperately with the mass of muddled paper in front of him, and then he brought a merciful end to his torment with the memorable words: 'Oh Christ.'

At this juncture I came calmly in as if that was the normal end to our rugby coverage, by saying: 'So much for today's rugby – now for today's racing results from three meetings.'

This was fine except that there were *four* meetings. So when three had been read, with more than a minute and a half of the programme still left, I started out on a long speech to close the programme, wondering how on earth I was going to make it last the allotted time, when I noticed the producer apparently having a fit next to me. Poor chap, I thought, it's all been too much for him. But as I talked on, I noticed that there seemed to be some rhyme and reason to his antics. For instance, he was softly muttering the words 'horses' and 'racing' and at the same time whipping himself in a very reasonable imitation of Lester Piggott riding out a close finish on Nijinsky.

At last it clicked. I stopped in my tracks and announced, to those members of the public who were still listening, that

there was of course still one more race meeting to come. It was duly read out at double speed and we managed to end the programme just on time. After this, such problems as tapes being put on at the wrong speed, and reporters failing to come up on the line when they are supposed to, seem relatively small.

Studios can be very frenetic places – indeed some producers seem to think it is necessary to whip up some crisis or panic even when there is no real cause, and it can be a trifle unnerving for the young and inexperienced. Nigel Starmer-Smith, now a popular and accomplished rugby commentator on B.B.C. Television, actually made his first broadcast on cricket. He was doing a round-up of the highlights of the day's county cricket, again a somewhat 'hairy' assignment, especially for someone not exactly *au fait* with all things cricketing. Poor Nigel was very nervous, as I noticed sitting opposite him. I read the scores and cued to him for the details, and in his excitement he began reading from the second page instead of the first. So his opening line was: 'Another good piece of bowling by Shackleton who took three for...' He stopped, then actually said (the only time I have heard it in earnest): 'I'm sorry, I'll read that again.'

Newsreaders are often rather stumped by sports items handed to them at the last minute and one famous gaffe was induced by a score from a Roses match in the 1930s: 'Now the close-of-play score in the Roses match at Headingley: Yorkshire 329 for four, Leyland 126, Hutton ill. Oh I'm sorry, Hutton 111.'

The real fun of broadcasting comes with the outside broadcast, especially the radio O.B. when the commentator has the thrill, the challenge and the responsibility of acting as the eyes of the listener. My very first live cricket broadcast was for the B.B.C. World Service (who put out a friendly, relaxed and informative programme every Saturday under the

convivial chairmanship of Paddy Feeney).
The game was between Surrey and
Yorkshire and Chris Old had just started
playing for the latter. I remember being
reasonably satisfied with my effort until the
moment I handed back to Paddy when I
said: 'The outstanding feature of the
morning has been the bowling of young
Old'. Paddy's quick response was: 'Oh, yes,
I remember his father, old Young'.

Such things are so easily said and
once out of the mouth cannot be retrieved.
Brian Johnston once remarked on a very
cold day at Northampton that the ground
was very deserted, in fact, there seemed to
be more cars there than people. It only
occurred to him afterwards to wonder how
the cars had got there! It was Brian too
who once inadvertently spoke of a fielder
at legslip with his legs wide apart, no
doubt 'waiting for a tickle'.

The Benson and Hedges
Cup Final of 1977 was a match
between Gloucestershire and Kent
and turned out to be one of the few
finals of the 1970s which Kent, having
reached Lord's, did not go on to win.
Gloucestershire had made a good score
and it was fairly apparent that
Kent were not going to make it
because the overs were fast
running out, and wickets were
falling. At one point Asif Iqbal,
of Kent and Pakistan, was out
and he was succeeded at the
wicket by John Shepherd, of Kent
and Barbados. 'The situation for
Kent', I told my listeners, 'is
looking blacker and blacker.'

Two years later the
Prudential World Cup opened
on a bitterly cold day with a match between
England and Australia at Lord's. It really
was bleak and we were glad to be inside a
warm commentary-box. I had made all
the obvious points about how many
sweaters the England fielders were
wearing and then I suddenly had a flash of

inspiration as to how I could convey just how bitter it was. 'You can see how cold it is out there now,' I observed, 'because the England fielders are putting their hands in their pockets between balls.'

Talking of flashes of inspiration, I apparently said at the end of one of those seemingly interminable floodlit one-day international matches in Australia: 'They are very aware of the enormous cost of the huge floodlights here at Sydney. There is also a local law that the lights must go out by half-past ten and, sure enough, the moment the match ended a short while ago, the lights went out *like a flash.*'

We get an amazing number of letters in the commentary-box, generally speaking friendly and appreciative ones. Some are also very interesting and some amusing, like the one from the housewife in August 1976 who wrote in professed disgust to say that she had been listening with her young and impressionable daughter to the commentary and 'I distinctly heard you saying "the bowler's Holding the batsman's Willey".' That was a leg-pull, I believe, but the best of these unintentional *double-entendres* was inevitably perpetrated by the life and soul of the commentary-box, Brian Johnston. He had to describe in one Test match that most delicate of cricketing matters, when a batsman gets hit where it hurts most. The batsman was Glenn Turner of New Zealand and the bowler Alan Ward of England. There was quite a delay whilst the England fielders all gathered round Turner, who was a bit shaken and needed a drink hastily summoned from the dressing-room. But he was eventually straightened out, so to speak, and Brian, who had described the injury with the utmost decorum, bearing his mixed audience in mind, took up the commentary again like this: 'So, he looks all right again. Alan Ward then to bowl to Turner; one ball left.'

On tour, other problems rear their heads. If things are going well for the team,

it is pleasant enough to tape interviews with the players. When things aren't going so well this can become an acute embarrassment. The producer says: 'Albert Brown in the *Daily Dredge* has written that there is bitter dissension within the team, Chris. Just do an interview with the captain about that will you? Oh, and ask him about the rumour that he's going to retire at the end of the tour because his form has been so disastrous . . . Don't be so soft on him this time, Chris.'

There were often desperately frustrating difficulties of a technical nature when it came to broadcasting from India. I spent three hours one Saturday in Jullunder trying to charm, persuade or cajole the studio engineer into getting me my line to London. I knew the concern which could be building up in the crowded sports studio in London – concern not for my plight but for the gap in the programme which would be created if my reports and interviews did not get through. At last I made some sort of contact on an echoing line: 'O.K.,' I said. 'I'll explain why I couldn't get through later. Let's not waste time. Here's my first report . . .'

'Hold it please Mr. Jenkins.' It was my friend the engineer, rushing into the studio looking very alarmed. 'Please,' he said, 'evacuate studio at once. Chief Minister of Punjab here to make ministerial broadcast.'

By the time he had done so, *Sports Report* had long gone off the air.

It was at Poona, I think, that I had the greatest difficulty in getting through, even though the secretary of the club there had kindly allowed one of his office boys to try to get the line through each lunchtime so that I could make a report to the early morning sports desk on Radio Four without having to miss the morning's play (the office, which had the only telephones, being well out of sight of the playing arena). Alas, the plan had been a more or less total failure and on the last day of the match, convinced it was due in part to the negligence or incompetence of the office boy, I was intending to tell him what I thought of him and Indian technology generally. As I brushed furiously past the main office desk I was handed a letter and fortunately I read it before I opened my tirade because it was from the offending youth himself and it began:

'Dear Mr. Christopher,
I am wishing to thank you, uncle, for your great kindness, superb hospitality and warm and sweet friendship to me . . .'

I did not finally boil over until much later on the tour. Whilst my Press friends had been sunning themselves by the beautiful pool at the Taj Mahal Hotel, I had been waiting for two hours beside a telephone with a report on the England team for the Fifth Test, which Tony Greig had kindly given me before its official announcement so that I could get it into the morning news bulletins at home. At last the line came through, just in time for the second edition of the *Today* programme.

'I've got the team,' I said with excitement.

'Sorry, mate,' said the chap presenting the sports news in London, 'there's so much soccer news here, there's no time for a cricket report.'

At that moment I felt like doing what the architect of the Taj Hotel had done on the day that his creation was officially opened. Realizing that they had misinterpreted his plans and built the hotel the wrong way round, he threw himself out of the window.

N

othing shapes the character of a game of cricket more fundamentally than the pitch.

Making a good one is hard work, requiring patience, endless rolling, a careful eye on the weather and a mixture of technical know-how, experience and good luck. Even when all goes well and a pitch is 22 yards of perfectly level, firm, closely cropped turf, things can go wrong. A couple of seasons ago at Worcester the start of a Championship match was delayed because the starting handle had fallen off the motor-roller and had been pressed deeply down into the pitch on a perfect length.

bowlers are equally unhappy. John Mortimore used to say of the Bristol wicket in his day that 'the only bowler it suits is a medium-paced dwarf.'

In 1981 England fell into line with the other countries by covering pitches at all times during matches when no play was in progress (except in fine weather in the intervals) thus depriving the game in England of some of its traditional variety and unexpectedness. Something of the mystique of reading a pitch was thus lost. Gone, temporarily at least, were the days when Wilfred Rhodes and Emmott Robinson of Yorkshire could disagree about the exact time when a wet pitch would start to take spin under the influence of hot sun.

It was on such a pitch that, in 1956, Jim Laker had taken his 19 wickets in the Old Trafford Test against Australia. It was England's nearest equivalent to the old 'Brisbane sticky' which used to occur first at Brisbane's Exhibition Ground and then at the Woolloongabba Ground, where tropical storms could make a mockery of a match. On one dramatic December day in 1950 Freddie Brown declared England's first innings at 68 for seven (Hutton not out eight) and Hassett counter-declared at 32 for seven (Bailey four for 22, Bedser three for nine) setting England 'only' 193 to win. Hutton, going in at number five made 62 not out, but the rest of England could score only 60. This was one of the times when, minutes after the storm broke, the stumps were swept away on a tide of water and floated to the boundary fence. On another occasion Sid Barnes, that incorrigible practical joker, took advantage of a hailstorm at the Gabba to amaze the England team still further by mounting the balcony above their dressing-room and dropping an enormous block of ice purloined from the refrigerator!

English cricketers tend to be suspicious of Australian 'curators', as the Australian groundsmen are called, and the

More often the weather intervenes and groundsmen, like farmers, are never satisfied. Nor, for that matter, are players. If a pitch is too damp or green, the batsmen complain louder than the seamers rub their hands. If it is too dry only the spinners are happy, and there are too few of them, especially at the highest level of cricket. If a 'hard, fast belter' is produced, bowlers of all types say it is impossible to get anyone out. If there is too much bounce the pitch is described as dangerous. If there is too little, it is impossible to play shots and the feeling is reciprocal. There was some evidence that the pitch was illegally watered during the Melbourne Test of 1954–55, although after *The Melbourne Age* had published Percy Beames's story the allegation was denied. Australians, similarly, were convinced that the Headlingley pitch was especially prepared for Derek Underwood in 1972, the occasion when fusereum disease spread on the Test strip because it had been covered during the wet weather preceding the match. On the 1974–75 tour England's players were firmly of the opinion that more grass than usual was being left on the Test pitches to suit the speed of Lillee and Thomson. The truth is that, at least in recent years, it has become common practice for groundsmen to shave off all the grass if the home sides have no fast bowling strength, as England have not had in recent years, and to leave it on if they have.

The most blatant example of this was at Calcutta in 1976–77 where the groundstaff were clearly to be seen, on the day before the game, down on their hands and knees rubbing out the last vestiges of grass with what appeared to be scrubbing brushes. If it was intended that the pitch should help the Indian spinners the plan was misconceived because it gave more assistance to England's faster bowlers, and the greater guile of Indian spinners on good pitches was wasted.

The most recent addition to Test match grounds is the Recreation Ground at St. John's, Antigua, where most of the hard work is done by prisoners from the gaol which stands on one side of what only a few years ago looked no more than a village ground. Hence the anguished reply made a few years ago to an English journalist's question: 'How many years have you been looking after this pitch?' 'Five years, man, *and I've still got five more to do.'*

The fact that the Antigua pitch is so good merely proves what any groundsman, however humble, will tell you, namely that it takes very hard labour to prepare a good pitch. Rolling is the essential base and it cannot be skimped, although the bent backs which always marked groundsmen in the old days were gained more from constantly searching their turf (outfields as well as pitches) for weeds and lifting each one that appeared out of the ground with a knife. Nowadays fertilizers and weedkillers take some of the backache out of the job, but although the end product may look prettier it is seldom so effective.

It is because they work so hard that groundsmen do not appreciate complaining cricketers. It was said of one of the Welsh county grounds, which shall be nameless, that the players were in far greater danger of catching silicosis than the miners. John Warr, indeed, remarked of a Welsh pitch that it needed a hoover not a mower. It was at Ebbw Vale that Norman Hill of Nottinghamshire, inspecting the pitch with Tony Lewis before the toss, remarked of the top dressing: 'Blimey, that's good-quality coal.'

In the same match, which the bowlers enjoyed more than the batsmen, Lewis angrily censored Peter Walker for getting out to a careless shot. 'It's alright for you,' replied Walker (who was born in South Africa), 'but when I tapped that pitch with my bat a moment ago, somebody tapped back from down below!'

You cannot play cricket without a pitch and thank goodness for the men – paid or voluntary – who prepare them. Theirs is one of the game's more thankless tasks yet it has its consolations and, no doubt, days when all the effort seems to have been worthwhile – when a pitch gives some help to the faster bowlers early in the game, permits plenty of runs for stroke-playing batsmen and some turn at the end for the spinners. Then everyone happily leaves the field of play: except, of course, the groundsman. The bowler's footmarks must be resown and another strip prepared. What a game!